AF575231

Joseph Beuys

Utopia at the Stag Monuments

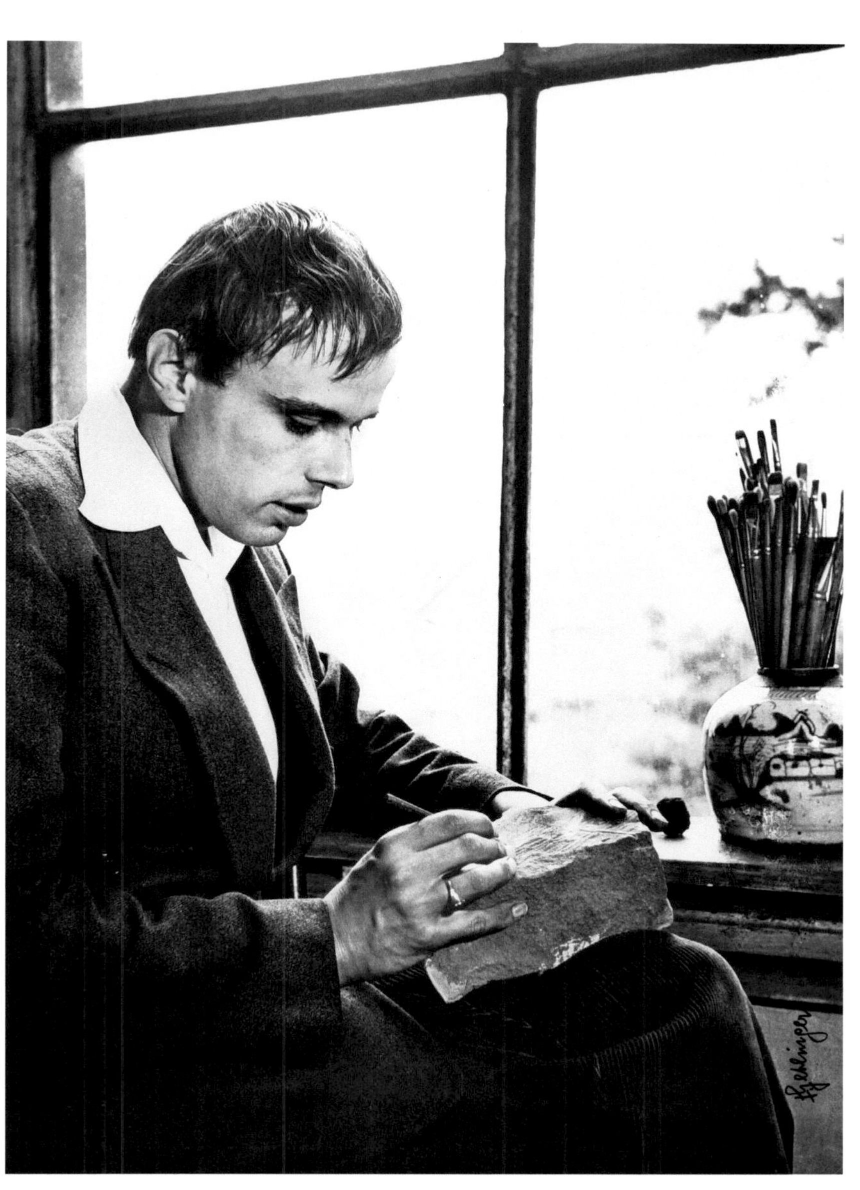

JOSEPH BEUYS
UTOPIA AT THE STAG MONUMENTS

GALERIE THADDAEUS ROPAC

Page 3
Fritz Getlinger, Joseph Beuys in the studio of Hanns Lamers in Koekkoek's Belvedere, 1950. Museum Kurhaus Kleve, Germany

Contents

Foreword

Joseph Beuys' radical thinking profoundly changed our understanding of art and set a new conceptual ground for generations of artists, notably through his concept of 'thought as form'. In a post-war context he developed the idea of art as a means of healing by exploring the power of materials and symbols, he defied pre-existing forms and expanded the notion of art through environments, performances, actions and public discussions. Curated by Norman Rosenthal, the exhibition *Utopia at the Stag Monuments* delves into Joseph Beuys' vision, tracing the development of his ideas. It can be seen through a retrospective lens, spanning the years 1947–1985, from his earliest rarely seen works – which offer precious hindsight into his iconography – to key sculptural moments and conceptual environments – all punctuated by his drawings, which crystallise his thinking.

The making of the exhibition was an ambitious project made possible thanks to our close collaboration with the Joseph Beuys Estate. Our first and most profound gratitude goes to Eva, Wenzel and Jessyka Beuys for their indispensable support, in-depth knowledge and encouragement. For the curation of the exhibition and his insightful essay, our particular thanks go to scholar Norman Rosenthal, who has been committed to investigating and exhibiting Joseph Beuys' work since the 1970s.

Our deepest thanks also go to those who agreed to lend works for the exhibition: The Joseph Beuys Estate, Anne and Anthony d'Offay, as well as Heiner, Céline and Aeneas Bastian and private collectors. My sincere gratitude also goes to Polly Robinson Gaer, Xaver von Mentzingen, Kelsey Corbett, Oona Doyle, Elizabeth Mercer, John Tiney, Marcus Rothe, Sarah Rustin, Francesca Andrews, Simon Dara and Frédéric Dahan.

Thaddaeus Ropac, London, April 2018

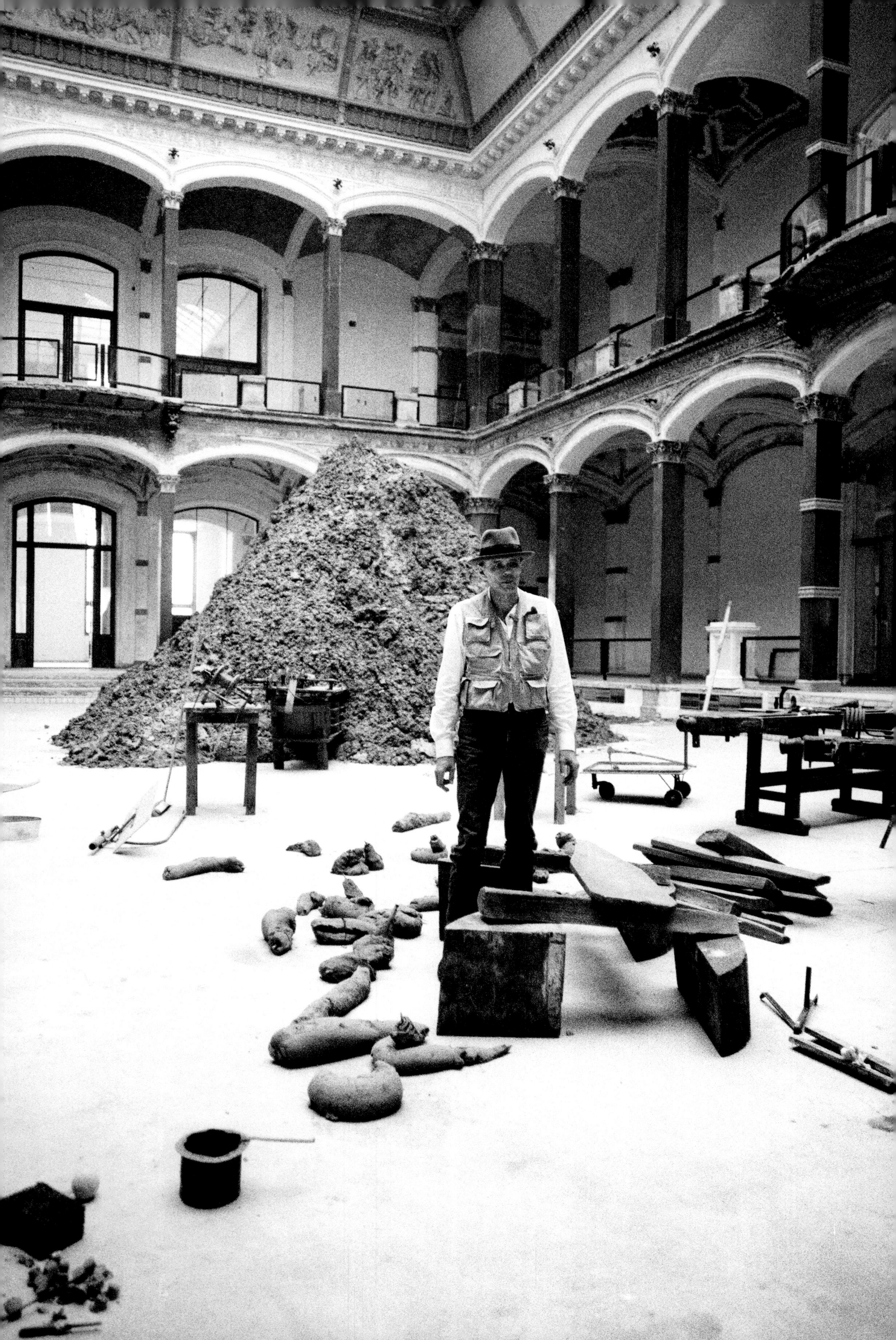

Joseph Beuys: Utopia at the Stag Monuments

Norman Rosenthal

Perhaps the most significant thing to say about Joseph Beuys is that he thought about and practised his art in a truly expanded field that never had less than a universal character. It was this that made him, and still makes him, controversial. Throughout his career he did everything he could to extend art beyond the narrow confines of a 'high art' that, especially since the decline of absolute belief systems, whether classical, monotheistic, Eastern or even Marxist, had ever-increasingly become a vehicle of bourgeois and petty capitalist values. As he himself often declared: 'Our culture is not moulded by culture but by economic power. There would be nothing wrong with that, if one had the right concept of economics in mind. We must get another notion of economics.'[1] The question when confronting a work of art by Beuys – or indeed the relics of his thought and actions that are in many ways self-consciously embedded in every one of his works, his sculptures, objects, drawings and souvenirs of his teaching practice and writing, such as blackboards – is to what extent the viewer-reader is able to 'have a presentiment of the things that are meant'.[2] Beuys did not necessarily expect complete understanding. Perhaps, indeed, there is no such thing. But his art and everything around his persona demanded empathy with the universality of the sciences and the arts as seen from a human historical perspective. This makes his work both demanding and yet ultimately hugely rewarding.

Such thoughts need to be present in our minds when confronting, for example, the relics of his studio in the installation *Hirschdenkmäler* [Stag Monuments].[3] First presented in spectacular fashion in 1982, it was central to the exhibition *Zeitgeist* at the Martin-Gropius-Bau in West Berlin which, at the time, had only just been rescued from near demolition. The museum was situated right by the Berlin Wall, and looking out from its windows one could easily observe the sandy

Joseph Beuys, *Zeitgeist*, Martin-Gropius-Bau, Berlin, 1982

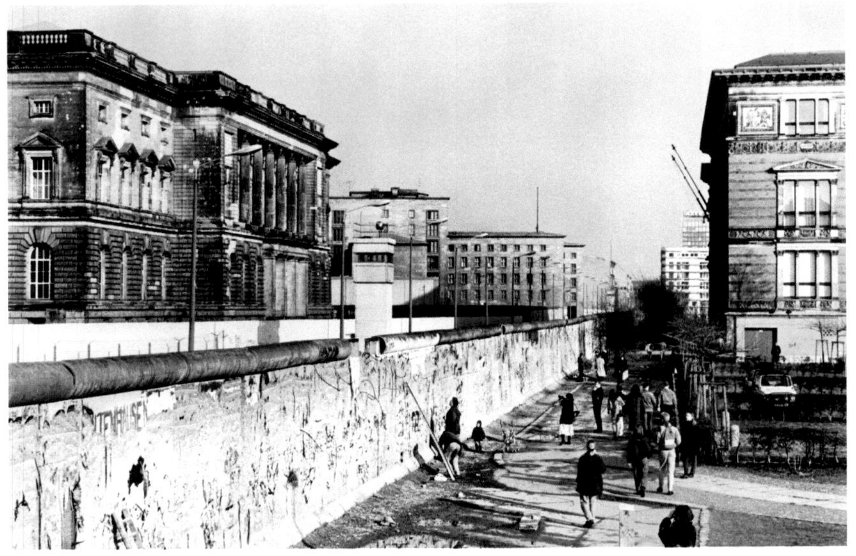

no man's land, like a kind of race track, that separated the political East from the political West, punctuated every few hundred metres by watchtowers (fig. 1). What once had been the centre – as it is now once again – was then at the edge. Beuys, like Andy Warhol and Jannis Kounellis, too, came to Berlin to look at this new spot loaded with scarred memory well before the exhibition opened to the public. Through their art, all succeeded in different ways in reflecting the history and the then-present circumstances of the site: Warhol made paintings that commemorated the light shows of National Socialist rallies in Berlin and Nuremberg and Kounellis made a heavy stone wall that blocked the windows of the gallery he was allocated.

Beuys, initially seemingly reluctantly, agreed to occupy the grandiose double-story central atrium of Wilhelmine grandeur around which the many large galleries of the museum had been constructed. After much thought, he decided, as he said himself, to 'bring all the contents of my Düsseldorf Studio to Berlin' (fig. 2). This was to include work benches, trollies, large unformed pieces of wood, an ironing board that had belonged to his mother, and at least two significant sculptures from the 1950s that had not left his possession and would now be given their sculptural tripods on which they, especially the clay woman known as *Torso*, now stand 'incomplete'. Incompleteness, or rather openness, is a characteristic of all of Beuys' work. Ideas that took the form of drawing at the very outset of his career often found more spectacular realisation only much later. Indeed, there is a pencil drawing with a moss rubbing addition (p. 134) that Beuys referred to as *Hirschdenkmal* [Monument to the Stag] dating to 1958. Another drawing, called *Am Hirschdenkmal* [By the Stag Monument], dated 1960, is an abstract composition on white card executed using only 'Braunkreuz'. Braunkreuz contains a mixture of industrial, animal and vegetable substances, but Beuys never revealed the exact components of that alchemical colour. The only time he spoke of it was in 1984: 'I was looking for a colour which was not at all experienced as a colour, which was a substance; let us say a kind of sculptural expression'.[4]

Figure 1
View of the Berlin Wall along the Niederkirchnerstraße with the Martin-Gropius-Bau, West Berlin (right) opposite the former Prussian Chamber of Representatives, East Berlin (left), January 1990

Figure 2
Ironing board used for *Hirsch* [Stag] and metal tools used for the *Urtiere* [Primordial Animals] in *Zeitgeist*, Martin-Gropius-Bau, Berlin, 1982

For Beuys drawing is rarely, if ever, just a sketch. Rather, it is, like all his works large and small, a representation of what he liked to call 'visual thinking'. Visual thinking, like his sculpture, delves deep into his own psyche as well as his very wide horizons of knowledge that encompass both human history and culture, as well as aspects of biology and physics with which he was familiar. There is a very real sense in which Beuys was always playing out, in his works as well as in his performative being, the all-knowing universal Faustian persona, now virtually unknown in this age of intense professional specialisation.

There is another sense in which all his work carries with it, through intense identification and empathy, the characteristic of self-portraiture, even when he – as he does so often – depicts the female figure in drawing. This is exemplified in the extraordinary figure of the woman on its tripod. *Torso* (1949/1951) was indeed a central element of the

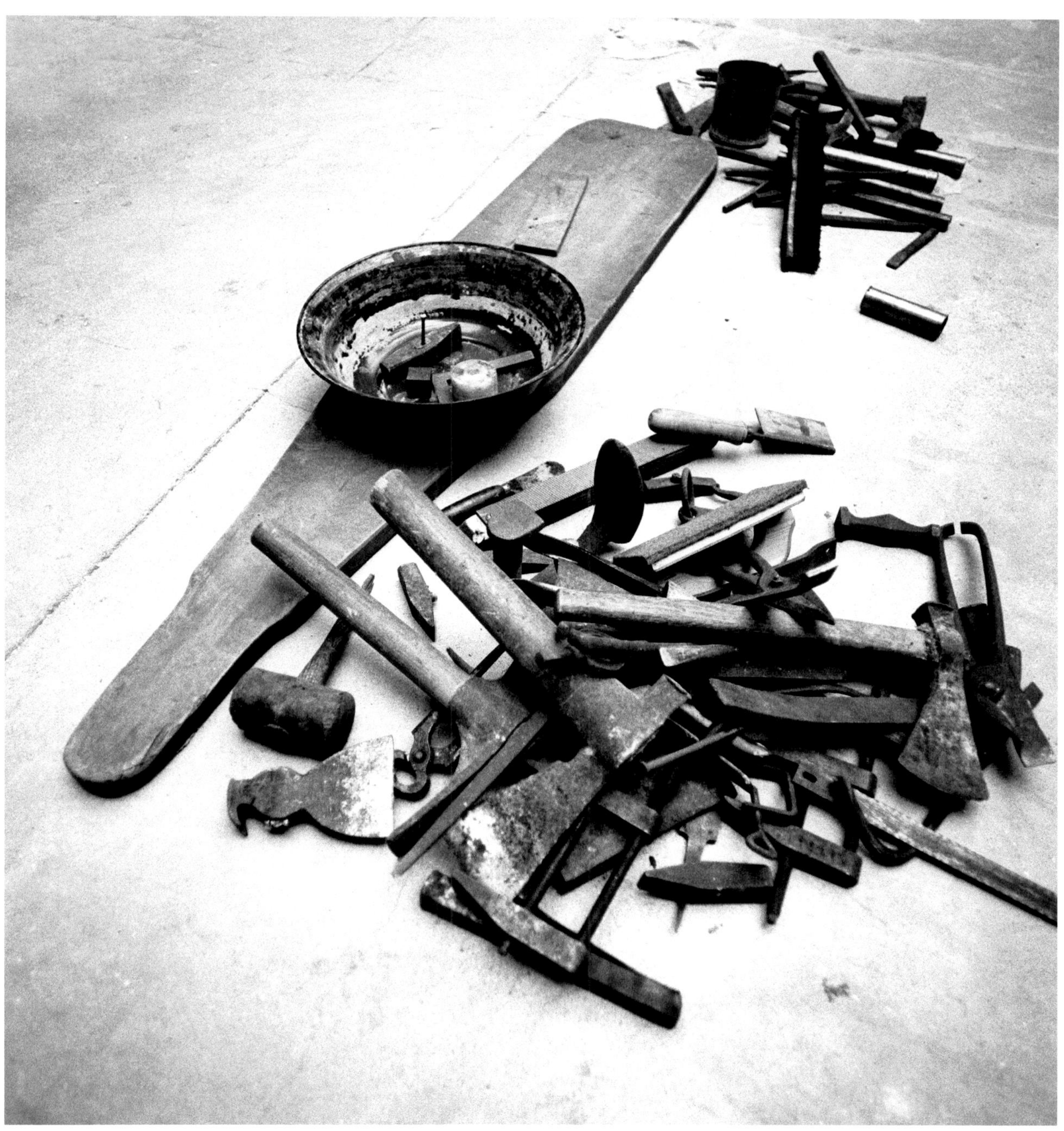

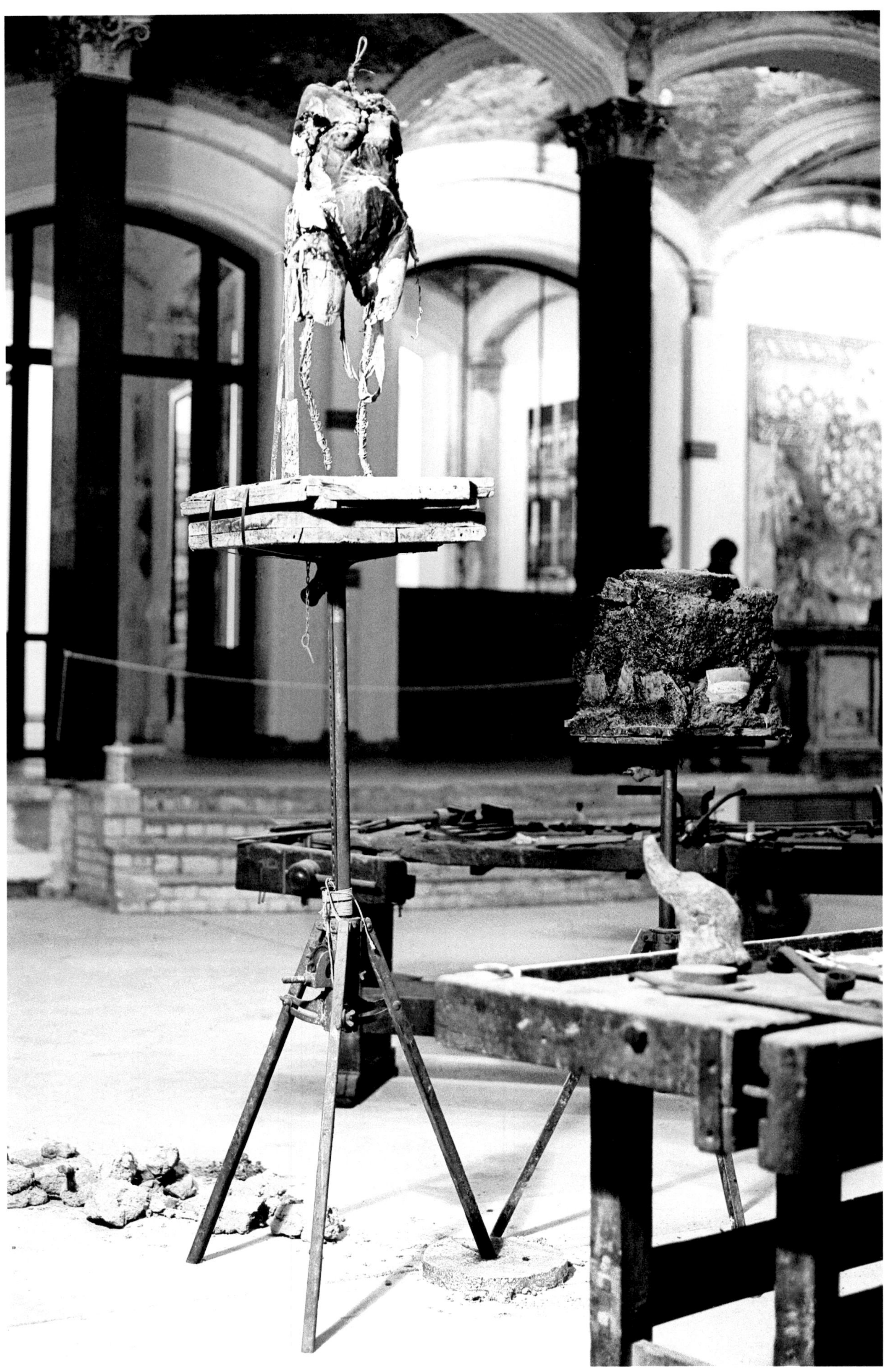

Stag Monuments installation in Berlin – a forceful queen-like counterpoint to the great mound of clay that was to become the dominating element in the grand atrium of the Martin-Gropius-Bau (fig. 3). A section of the mound was transformed into the bronze *Blitzschlag* [Lightning] sculpture that Beuys had cast after the completion of the *Zeitgeist* exhibition at a foundry in Berlin, and which became the dominating part of a new bronze and aluminium cast environment called *Blitzschlag mit Lichtschein auf Hirsch* [Lightning with Stag in its Glare] (1958–85). The incompletion of the female figure that had been in Beuys' studio since the 1950s is an affirmation of the poetic and open-ended creativity that remains the essential aspect of his lifetime's work.

The female figure was never cast – probably, one suspects, because of its fragility. Only the male element was cast, an object made of a cubic earth element mounted on a tripod and surmounted by a simple compass. Beuys called this *Boothia Felix* (fig. 4). Named after a strip of land in Northern Canada where, back in 1831, the Magnetic North Pole had first been established, he intended it as a human register of the metaphysical sculptural landscape he had constructed

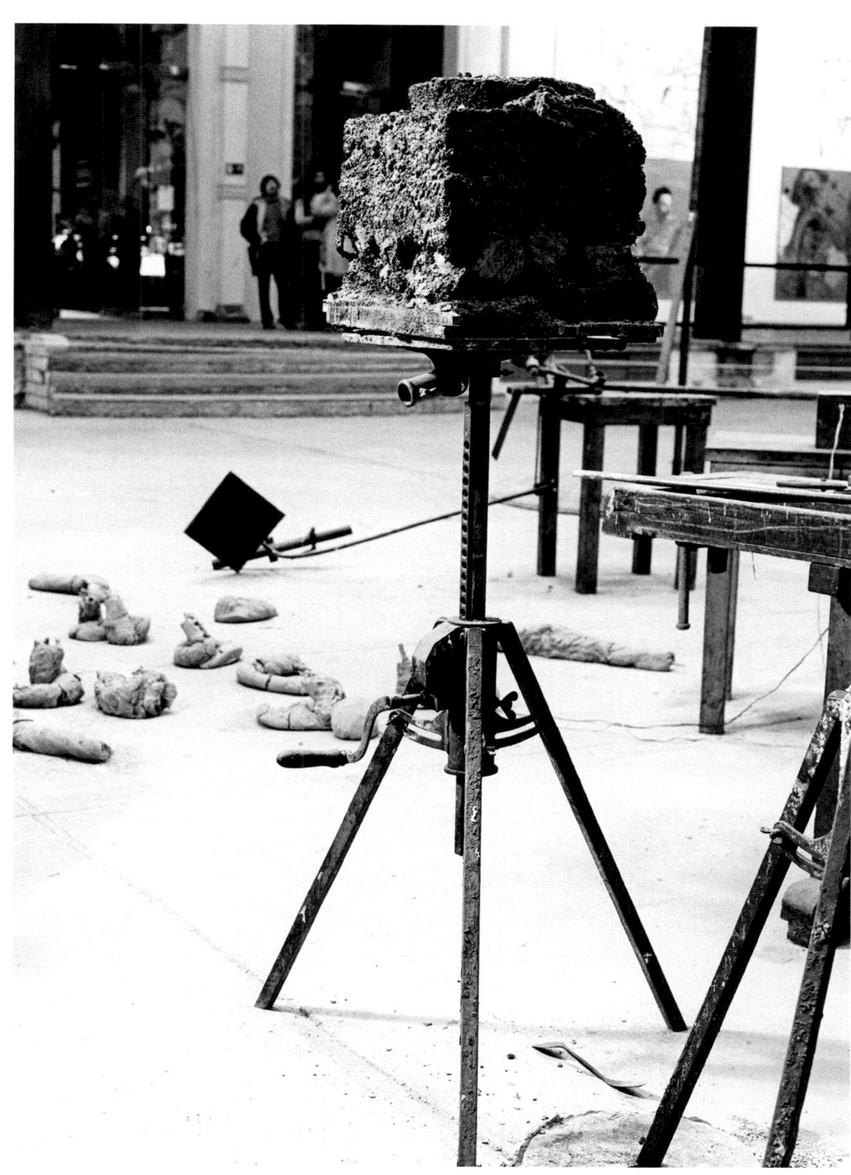

Figure 3 (opposite)
Torso in *Zeitgeist*, Martin-Gropius-Bau, Berlin, 1982

Figure 4
Boothia Felix in *Zeitgeist*, Martin-Gropius-Bau, Berlin, 1982

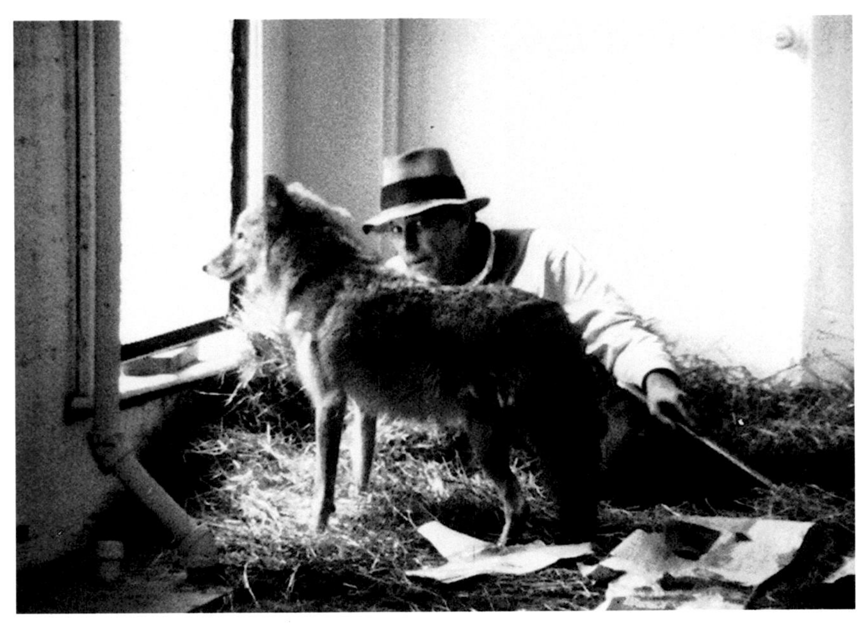

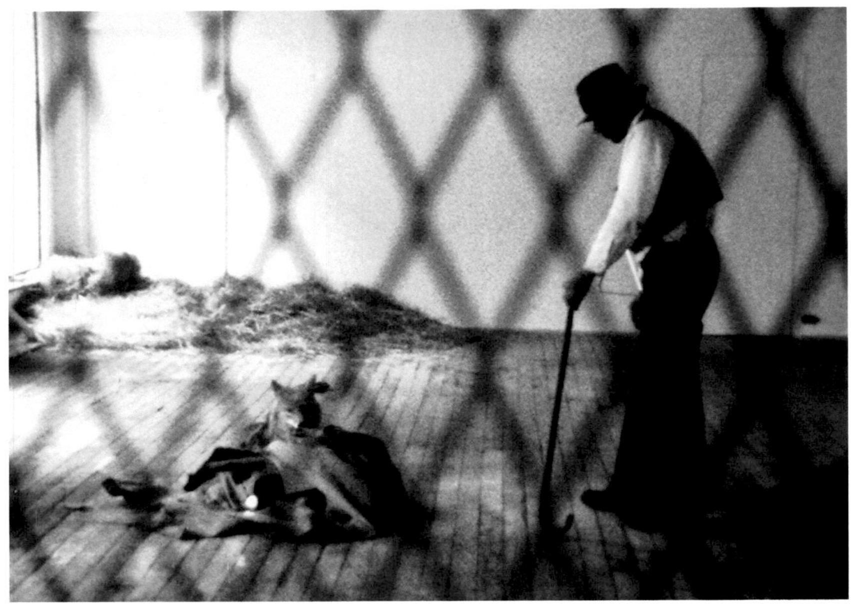

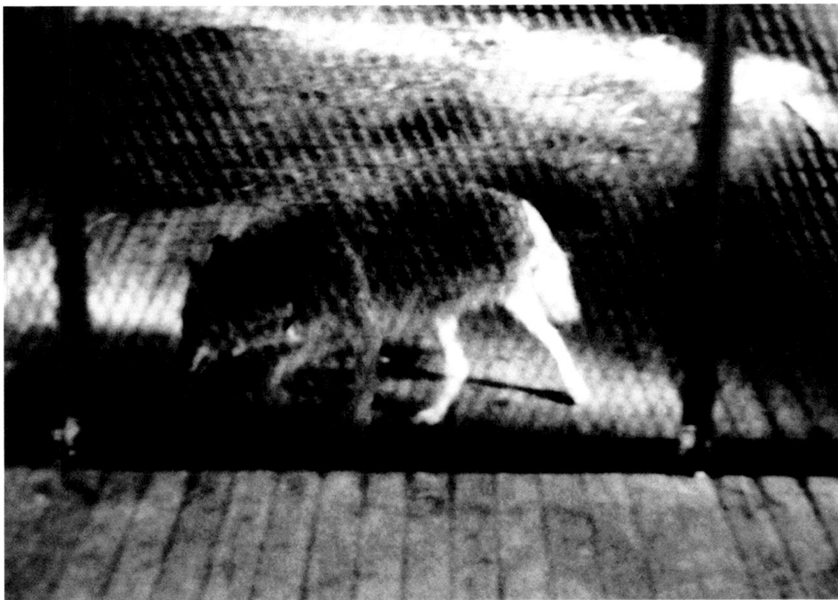

Figures 5, 6 & 7
Joseph Beuys, *I Like America and America Likes Me*, 1974. Stills from 16mm film by Helmut Wietz

to survive the temporality of the exhibition in Berlin in 1982. Such dramatic landscapes that Beuys invented using both performative and sculptural elements – one could include moments such as *Iphigenie* or *Richtkräfte* [Directive Forces], originally performed during a month-long continuous lecture at the Institute of Contemporary Arts, London, in 1974, or for that matter the even more visionary presentation of the artist wrapped in a large felt blanket living with the Coyote in a New York gallery, also of 1974 – all have hermetic and subjective aspects about which one can but speculate (figs. 5, 6 & 7).

The exhibition *Scythians: warriors of ancient Siberia*[5] at the British Museum provided an occasion to meditate on the history of central Eurasia stretching back over thousands of years, from the Crimea north and eastwards over massive areas where humans and animals, sometimes bound together in common fates and destinies, migrated and established sophisticated evolutionary cultures. We learn about materials that have been excavated in recent centuries from artificial mounds found across the areas occupied by Scythians that are not dissimilar to the clay mound Beuys made as the site of the *Stag Monuments*. It was in these mounds, as is the case with all ancient cultures, that they chose to bury their regal dead and to provide them with sufficient provisions for their assured afterlife. Perhaps today only true artists have access to this afterlife, but then, of course, for Beuys every human being had the potential to be an artist – that was the central aspect of his 'revolutionary economic' theory that, if enacted, would transform our society.

'Scythians' was of course a generic name in use – at least since the time of Herodotus in the 5th century BCE – for the many largely nomadic tribes that over many centuries occupied areas that stretched from the Black Sea to Northern China. They were inevitably often at war with each other, as well as with the worlds of ancient Greece and Persia. It was Herodotus, arguably the first objective Western historian in a 'modern' sense, who first described these people. For him, they were barbarians, but he described them as having a sophisticated material culture. In the fourth volume of the *Histories*, he writes of what are now classic Beuysian materials, such as felt, fat and blood, as well as more obvious materials, such as wood and cast metals, both base and precious, including gold (figs. 8, 9 & 10, pp. 18–19).

Many of Herodotus' descriptions, taken down almost five hundred years before the Christian era, have, astonishingly, been confirmed by the material archaeology conducted over the last hundred years and more. Thus it seems, if it even matters, more plausible that when Beuys was shot down from his Fokker plane over the Crimea that his unconscious body was covered 'in fat to help it regenerate warmth and wrapped in felt as an insulator to keep the warmth in'.[6] It was to become the Saul/Paul moment for the young soldier, who had however, at least in his later autobiographical imagination, been organising manifestations that he was to call 'exhibitions' since his birth in Cleves in 1921, which he describes as 'a wound drawn together with plaster'.[7]

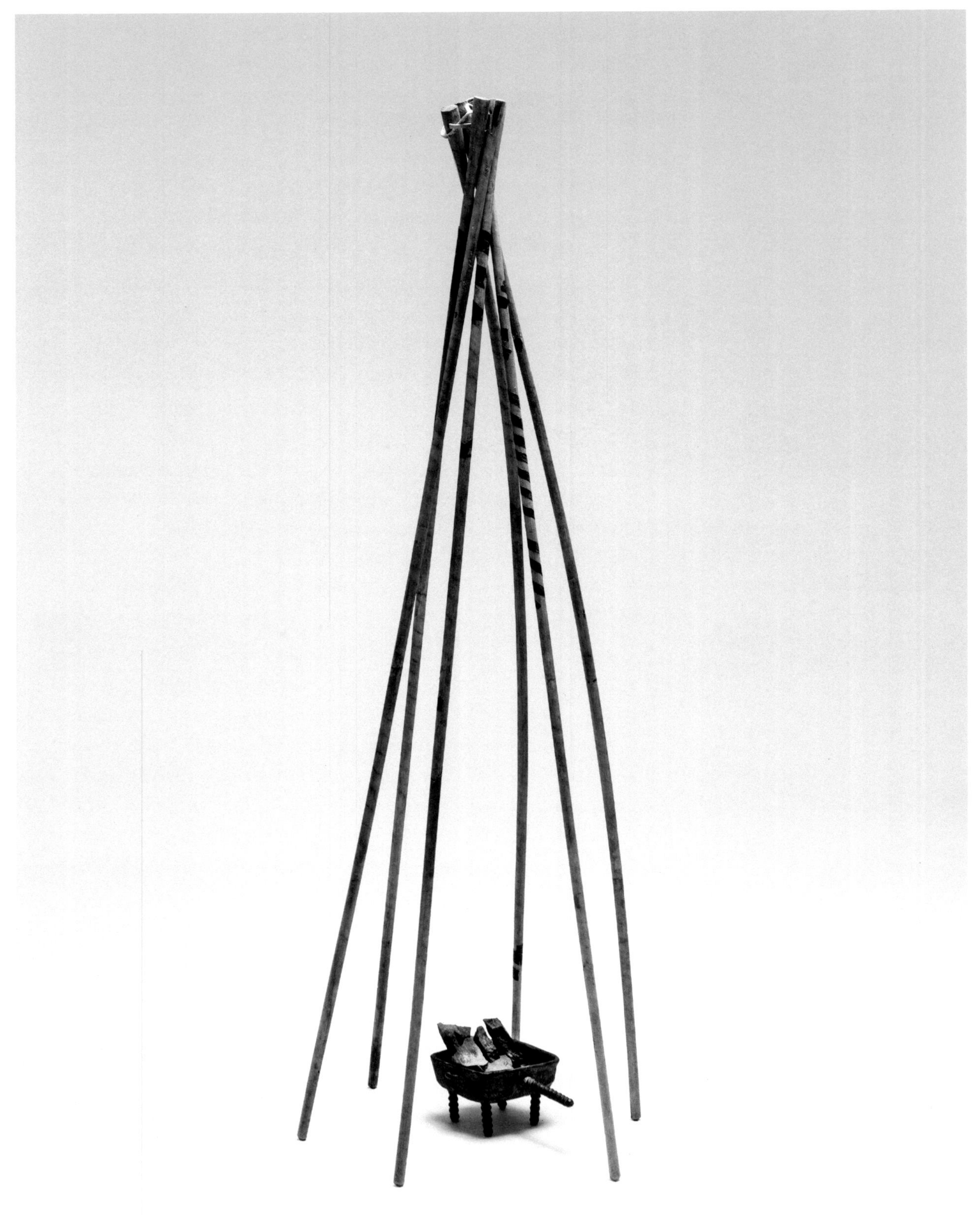

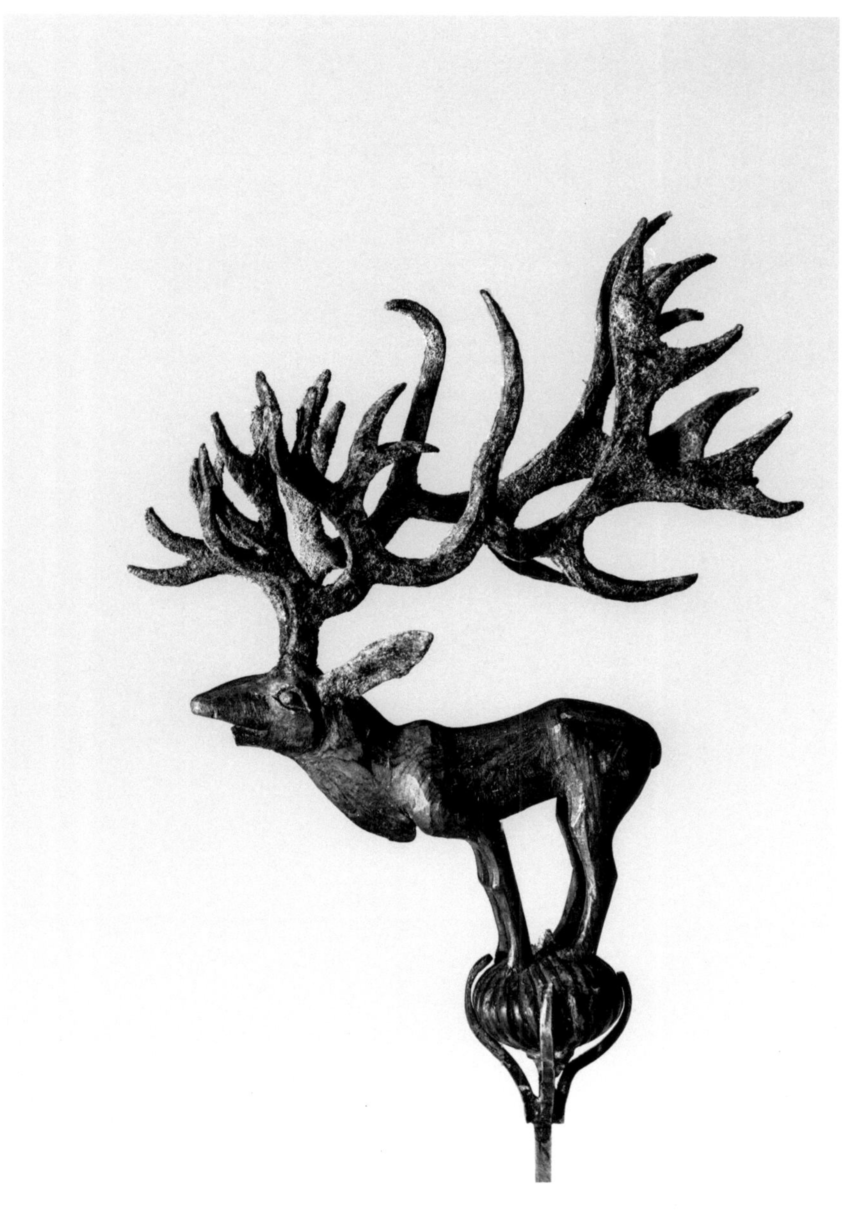

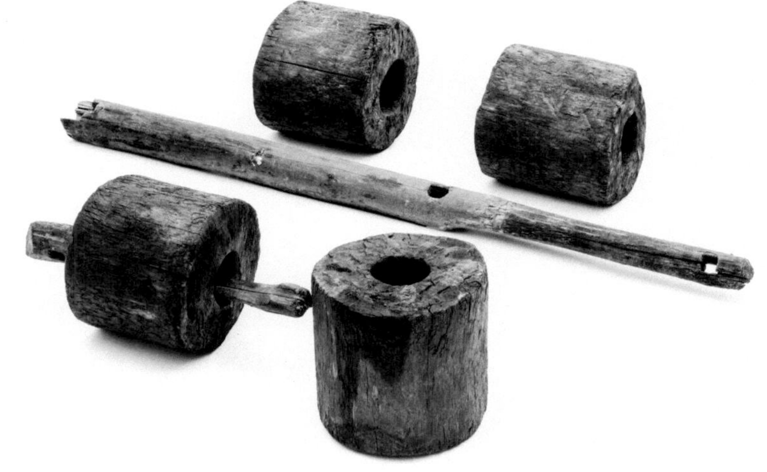

Scythian artefacts from burial mounds at Pazyryk, Altai Mountains, southern Siberia. State Hermitage Museum, St Petersburg

Figure 8 (opposite)
Hexapod stand: six sticks of a smoking tent frame and brazier, found with fragments of a felt cover, burial mound 2, Pazyryk, late 4th–early 3rd century BCE

Figure 9 (above)
Wooden pin finial in the form of a stag on a ball, burial mound 2, Pazyryk, 5th century BCE

Figure 10 (right)
Scythian wheels and axle of a heavy wagon, burial mound 5, Pazyryk, 3rd century BCE

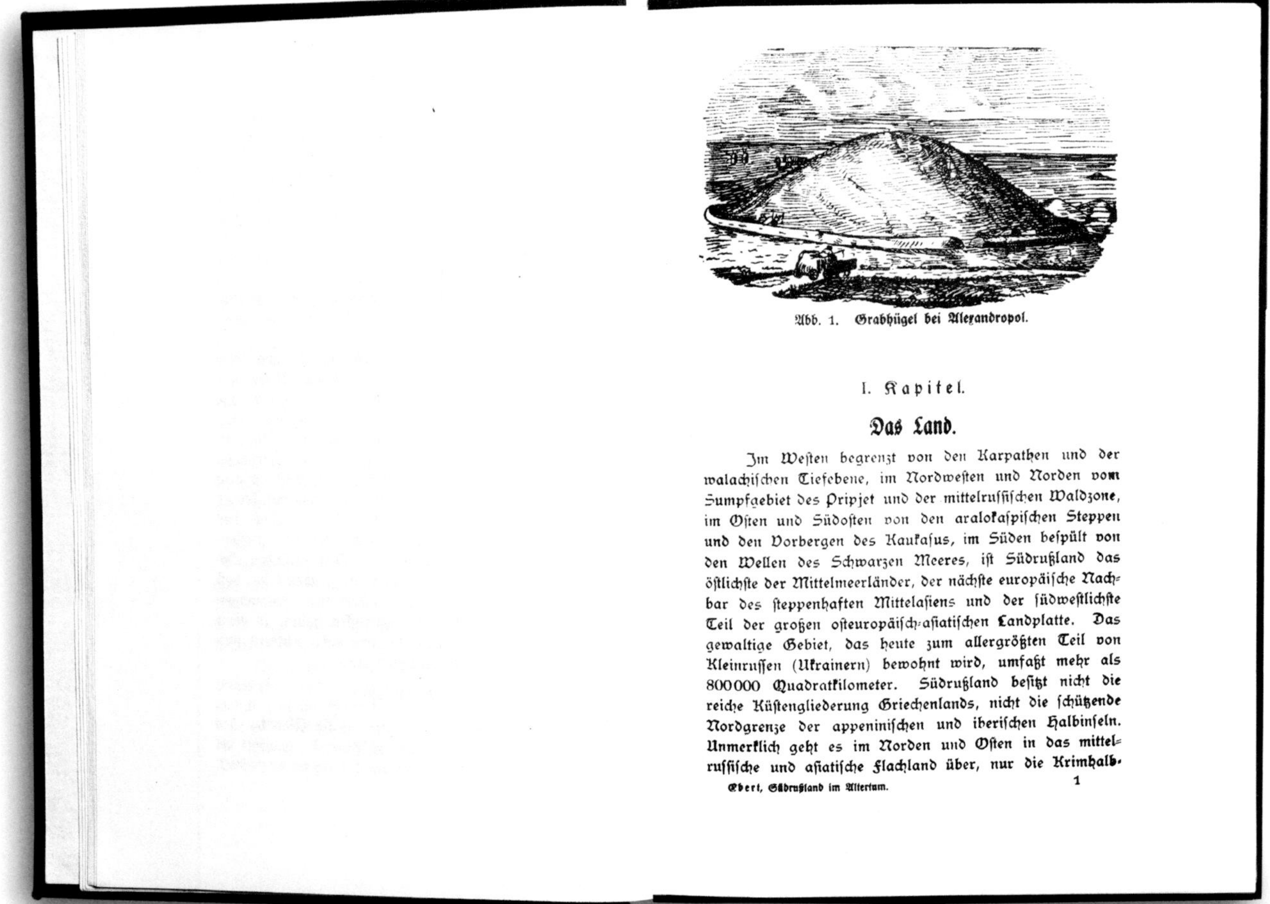

Abb. 1. Grabhügel bei Alexandropol.

I. Kapitel.

Das Land.

Im Westen begrenzt von den Karpathen und der walachischen Tiefebene, im Nordwesten und Norden vom Sumpfgebiet des Pripjet und der mittelrussischen Waldzone, im Osten und Südosten von den aralokaspischen Steppen und den Vorbergen des Kaukasus, im Süden bespült von den Wellen des Schwarzen Meeres, ist Südrußland das östlichste der Mittelmeerländer, der nächste europäische Nachbar des steppenhaften Mittelasiens und der südwestlichste Teil der großen osteuropäisch-asiatischen Landplatte. Das gewaltige Gebiet, das heute zum allergrößten Teil von Kleinrussen (Ukrainern) bewohnt wird, umfaßt mehr als 800000 Quadratkilometer. Südrußland besitzt nicht die reiche Küstengliederung Griechenlands, nicht die schützende Nordgrenze der appeninischen und iberischen Halbinseln. Unmerklich geht es im Norden und Osten in das mittelrussische und asiatische Flachland über, nur die Krimhalb-

Ebert, Südrußland im Altertum. 1

As a teenage boy in his formative years, he could not help being caught up in all the terrifying perversions of that German history and culture that was to turn European civilisation upside down and from which, in 1945, recovery was to seem like a near-impossibility. One fact, however, that seems more than plausible was that he was a voracious reader of books, some of which he seems, as he claimed, to have obtained by rescuing them from the notorious book burnings that took place all over Germany, not just in Berlin, from as early as 1933. As to which scientific books Beuys was reading at this time, whether banned or not, we can but speculate. A near-contemporary popular book on the Scythians by Max Ebert (1879–1929), *Südrußland im Altertum*, first published in 1921, is still considered a serious contribution to the subject. It opens with a vignetted illustration of the Alexandropol 'Grabhügel' [Grave Mountain], which could be in present-day Gyumri, Armenia (fig. 11). It was one of the kind that might have been visible to Herodotus, but was also common across the Ukrainian and Russian Steppes, including in Pazyryk in the high Altai region of Central Siberia – the latter geographical nomenclature meaning 'gold mountain'. As Beuys describes his *Stag Monuments* in a manifesto written for the *Zeitgeist* exhibition catalogue, they 'are accumulation machines at which human beings and all other spirits meet, in order to work together [...] and out of which after the terrible making-dead we will re-awaken the planet to life'.[8]

Figure 11
Opening page of Max Ebert, *Südrußland im Altertum* [South Russia in Antiquity], 1921, with an illustration of the Alexandropol grave mountain

So how are we meant to understand Beuys' cryptic, yet concise description? It seems to suggest a past, in other words a long history, stretching back into the most distant human times. Equally, it is a human-made present with all its attendant political problems, a present that speaks to our times, whether it be the terrifying world of Ghouta in Syria, or the homeless transient people sleeping on streets all over Europe. Yet, Beuys also posited an ultimately optimistic future for humankind that he thought possible through his own concept of art as a transformative mechanism towards positive possibilities. Beuys' entire iconography and its attendant open-ended formal and – for want of a better phrase – stylistic handwriting make all his work, whether on a large ambitious scale or as small as a humble postcard, instantly recognisable.

Few, if indeed any, artist-poets in the post-1945 era, indeed arguably of any era, have so intensively incorporated in their persona or work the concept of the Fisher King. Beuys was a latter-day Parsifal figure, wearing his fishing jacket that was as much a part of his symbolic outfit as the famous hat that disguised the head wound he sustained when he was shot down. Indeed, Beuys' world had been very much 'The Waste Land' that T.S. Eliot had prophesied in the last lines of his great poem, first published in 1922, and is itself riddled with intentional ambiguities, as well as cross-cultural and historical referencing. The very last line of the poem is a simple Sanskrit prayer for peace that in Eliot's own words 'passes all understanding'. Even when quoting Dante, Eliot speaks of Goodness as it guides you to the summit of the stairway, we should be also mindful of pain.

I sat upon the shore
Fishing, with the arid plain behind me
Shall I at least set my lands in order?
London Bridge is falling down falling down falling down
Poi s'ascose nel foco che gli affina
Quando fiam ceu chelidon — O swallow swallow
Le Prince d'Aquitaine à la tour abolie
These fragments I have shored against my ruins.
Why then Ile fit you. Hieronymo's mad againe.
Datta. Dayadhvam. Damyata.
Shantih shantih shantih

The Indian mantra is not unlike Beuys' own famous chant of 1968, the year of student revolutions, *Ja Ja Ja Ja Ja, Nee Nee Nee Nee Nee*, the *Veränderungskonzert* [Concert of Changes] that he was to transform into a multiple.

What aesthetic or political answers lie within the works? These begin with the surprisingly characteristic early bronze crosses from 1949 (figs. 12 & 13 overleaf) made very much under the influence of some of his teachers at the Düsseldorf Academy of Art, who included

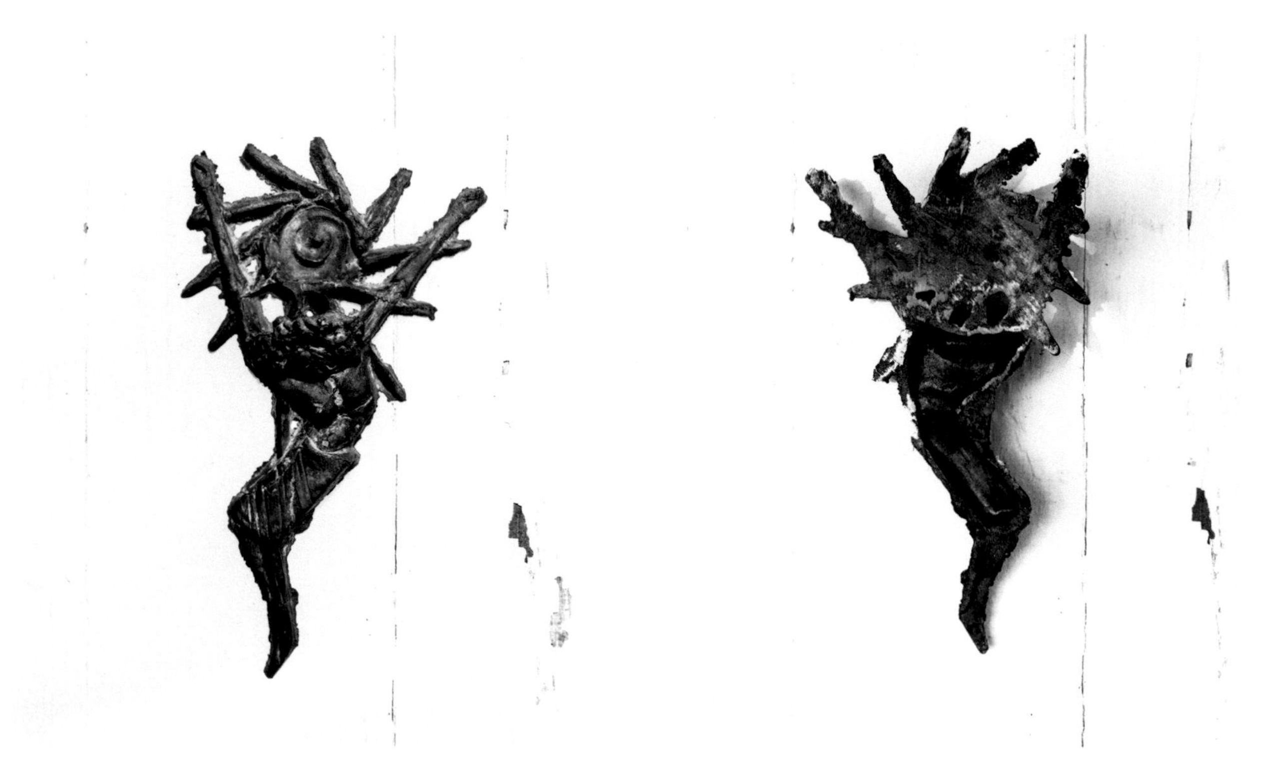

Figures 12 & 13
Joseph Beuys, *Gekreuzigter Christus (mit Sonne)*
[Crucified Christ (with Sun)], 1949
(back and front)

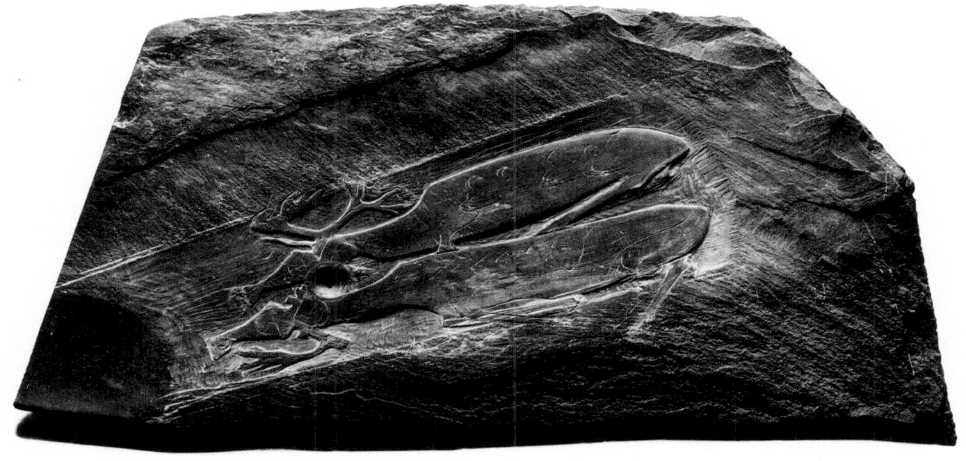

Figure 14
A carved slate with two stags (ca. 1949) by Joseph Beuys photographed by Fritz Getlinger in the *Kleve 1950–1961* portfolio

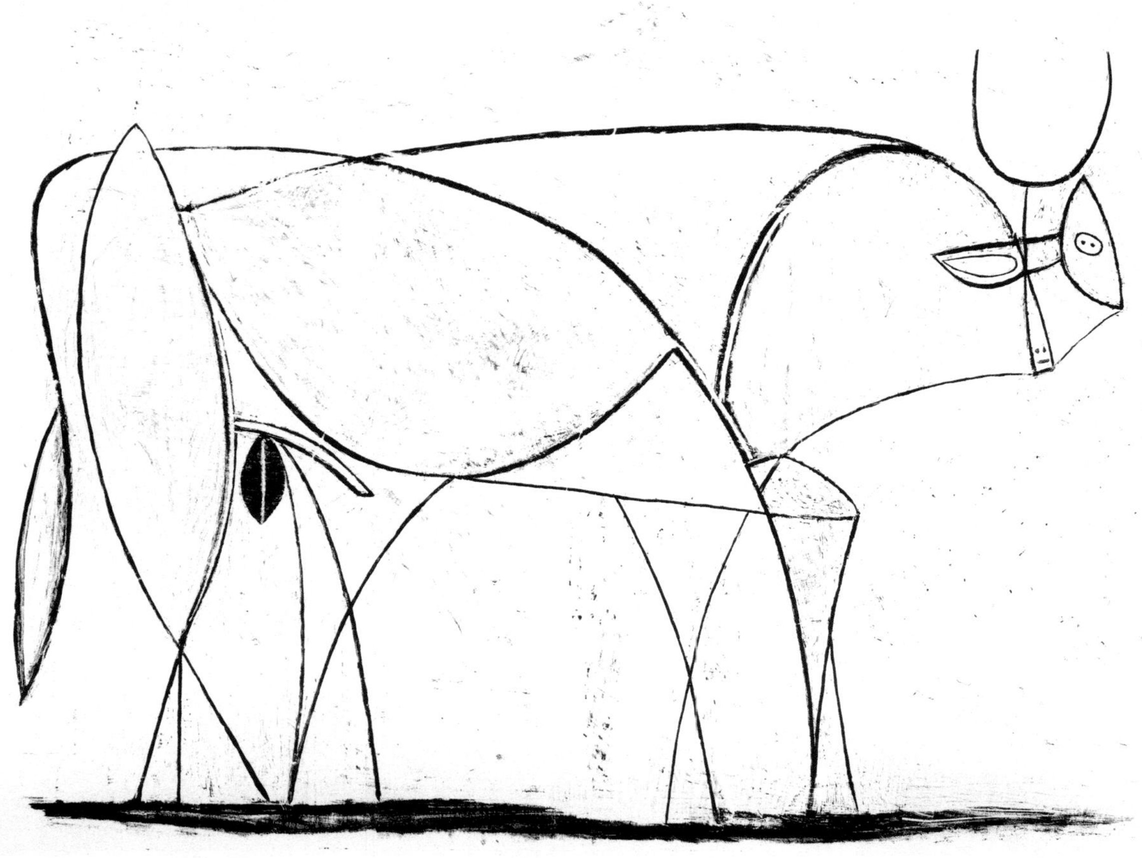

Joseph Enseling (1886–1957). After the Second World War, Ewald Mataré (1887–1965) found himself engaged, sometimes with the help of Beuys, who must have been a favourite pupil, as evidenced in the photographic images to be found in the *Kleve Portfolio*, in the redecoration of Catholic Churches from Cologne to Salzburg, so many of which had been devastatingly damaged during the war. There was now a need for new meaningful symbolic and iconographical symbols to replace those dating from the Middle Ages through to recent modern times. They required replacing and above all reimagining, whether as bronze doors or, for that matter, crucifixes.

Beuys' teachers were also artists for whom the depiction of animals was important, and it could be argued that the centrality of the animal in Beuys' own work owes much to their influence. Mataré, in particular, had sought and found a Germanic translation of Picasso's own notion of the animal, one which Beuys expanded to a universal level, and which allows us to reflect more generally on the affinities between himself and the great Spanish master of the first half of the 20th century (figs. 14 & 15).

In spite of *Guernica* (1937), Picasso is not usually thought of as a political artist, rather the reverse. However, his sensitivity to both the joys and the tragedies of his own times as they evolved throughout his long lifetime of making art was indeed profound and can easily be demonstrated. As well as being a social commentator, Beuys was an artist with a profound sense of humour and irony. Furthermore,

Figure 15
Pablo Picasso, *Le taureau* [The Bull], 5 January 1946, 9th state lithograph. Musée national Picasso, Paris

the ability of Picasso to instantly imagine a sculpture out of a down-to-earth, ordinary object lying around – for instance the classic bicycle stool that 'becomes' the head of a bull – is Beuysian in a way that has more affinity than with the conceptually inclined Duchamp, with whom he is more often compared. In that sense, Beuys was never really narrowly a conceptual artist. His works strive much more towards a subjective, even expressionist, universalism that allows viewers to bring into play their own personal history and frames of reference. Beuys' use of felt is a case in point. That felt represented warmth for him is well known, and is evidenced by the *Feldbett* [Campaign Bed] (1982) (pp. 82–83) that also formed part of the *Stag Monuments* where, alongside the *Hirsch* [Stag], the *Ziege* [Goat], and the *Urtiere* [Primordial Animals] also known as *Lehmlinge*, we can imagine the artist himself wrapped in felt.

Felt is a unique unwoven material that, in its early forms, was fabricated from closely pressed animal hair. It is even thought that it might have been invented as a kind of side effect when the hair of animal skins, used by primitive humans for warmth, began matting with the sweat of the body against which they were pressed. Felt formed itself, then, through what one might describe as automatic generation – itself a very Beuysian cultural concept. 'Felting' is also a verb – in other words, a process of becoming that is central to the Beuysian sense of human evolution. This evolution extends back to the mythical moment when God accepted more readily the sacrifice of the 'firstlings of his flock and the fat thereof', which Abel was to offer before he was murdered by his older brother Cain. Iphigenie, with whom Beuys also identified in his famous performance in Frankfurt in 1969, was indeed about to be sacrificed to the goddess Artemis, when, in the last moment, a stag was offered in her place and she was sent by her brother Orestes to Tauris, in what is present-day Crimea.

Beuys, like almost every great artist, is able to get into the character of the opposite sex – as can be seen in so many of his drawings and the several early sculptures of pregnant women in the current exhibition. In its own way, *Torso* was itself a kind of self-portrait, which came with him to Berlin to be part of the *Stag Monuments* environment. Beuys had this extraordinary capacity to renew and transform, both within his own creativity and equally by creating new myths out of ancient ones. Time, for him, was equally a great and vital transformer. The feminine *Infiltration-homogen für Cello* [Infiltration-homogeneous for Cello] (p. 71), covered in felt, was, in Beuys' own words, an instrument equivalent to the grand piano, which 'becomes an homogeneous deposit of sound with the potential to filter through the felt'.[9] It was originally made for the now legendary Fluxus performance artist/musician Charlotte Moorman (1933–1991), with 'the red crosses signifying emergency that threatens if we stay silent and fail to make the next evolutionary step'.[10]

Noise and music, on the one hand, and silence on the other, form another of Beuys' constant amalgam of opposites enacted in the *Stag Monuments*. Beuys himself urged in its presence: 'I will scream:

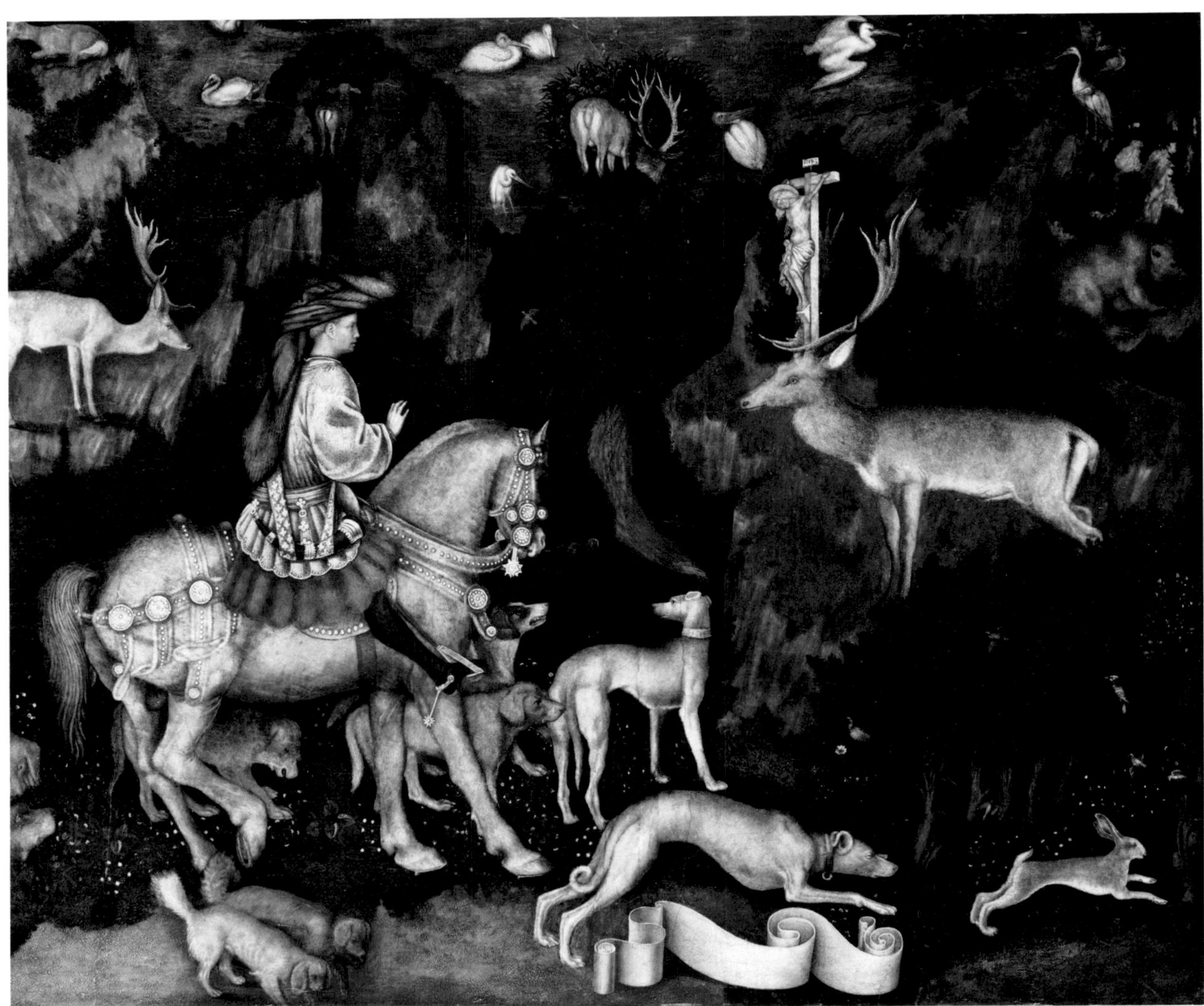

Figure 16
Pisanello, *The Vision of Saint Eustace*, ca. 1438–42, egg tempera on wood. The National Gallery, London

there will no longer be any useful sculpture down here if the SOCIAL ORGANISM AS A LIVING BEING is not also here.'[11] Sculpture may be silent as we look at it, but for Beuys the 'coming together' of humankind with all its history and memory with nature – echoing Saint Eustace in the forest, where the stag's antlers became a vision of the crucifixion (fig. 16) – brings dialogue and therefore sound and music to the visual.

Indeed, all the five classical senses are enlisted by Beuys in his work. There is the ever-present smell of honey, but also stale margarine and tallow fat, as well as chocolate and blood. As Beuys wrote, the *Stag Monuments* were 'proof that the Idea is real and that the theory of entropy is false'.[12] From the early crosses born out of the disasters of the Second World War, or the sense of pride that emanates so obviously from the *Tierfrau* [Animal Woman] of 1949/1979 (pp. 40–41), to energising works such as *Kleines Kraftwerk* [Small Power Station] of 1984 (pp. 64–69), where the idea of abstracted energy meets the idea of abstracted form, his art is forever a manifestation of a fundamental optimism that runs through all of his works and performances, large and small in their realisation. The work of Beuys thus becomes a reflection of a kind of universal optimism, even as he overcame a period of personal depression in the early 1950s from which he ultimately emerged. A psychological necessity in the years that followed the destructions and the traumas that were the inevitable by-products of the disastrous periods of European wars of the 20th century had put into question the whole project of European culture as it had been understood.

But it needed to transcend a simplistic optimism, which had occasioned concepts such as 'Zero Hour', that wanted to sweep all away and start again as though nothing had happened. Ernst Bloch (1885–1977), who had managed to escape to America during the period 1933–1945, composed a vast three-volume survey of European utopian cultural potential in spite of everything. Under the rubric *The Principle of Hope*, he gave voice to the necessity, as he put it at the very beginning of his magnum opus, of 'learning hope' which, for him, was 'superior to fear [...] neither passive like the latter, nor locked into nothingness'.[13] From the perspective of art this was of course a rejection of the abstract, yet equally it was not, as such, an acceptance of Platonic perfection as it had been understood and striven for by European culture hitherto. It required, he later wrote, 'the crucial difference and the crucial truth' that:

> all great art shows the pleasant and homogeneous aspects of its work-based coherence broken, leafed open by its own iconoclasm, wherever immanence is not driven to closedness of form and content, wherever it still poses as 'fragment-like' [...] and it is precisely in this space that the 'aesthetic-utopian' meanings of the beautiful, even the sublime, make their presence felt.[14]

Like most of his philosophical contemporaries Bloch believed in Marx and his theories of knowledge and economics, but above all, like Beuys, he also felt that knowledge needed to be 'related not only to what is past but essentially to what is coming up'.[15] Ultimately, contained within each work of Beuys is a miraculous fusion of past and present, which also becomes a manifesto of hope for the future. His art, like the philosophy of Bloch, represents a theory of knowledge that also strives with hammer-like force (p. 93) to transcend theories based on just materialism.

More necessary is a sense of 'life, consciousness, the switch from quantity to quality, Novum and dialectics as a whole' to replace what he describes as the 'God hypothesis'.[16] A sense of 'quality', even when it came to judging the *Height of the Berlin Wall* in 1964 – that its height might be extended by five centimetres but retain better proportion and form – was always of central importance for Beuys. His drawings and the sculptures he translated from found objects or formed with clay, bronze or copper were never less than exquisite and dramatically perfectly calibrated – just because at one level they represent spontaneous and free thought, from the *Kreuze* [Crosses] (pp. 46–47) to the *Filzanzug* [Felt Suit] (p. 73) multiple, *Thor's Hammer* to the ironing board that 'becomes' the body of the *Stag*.

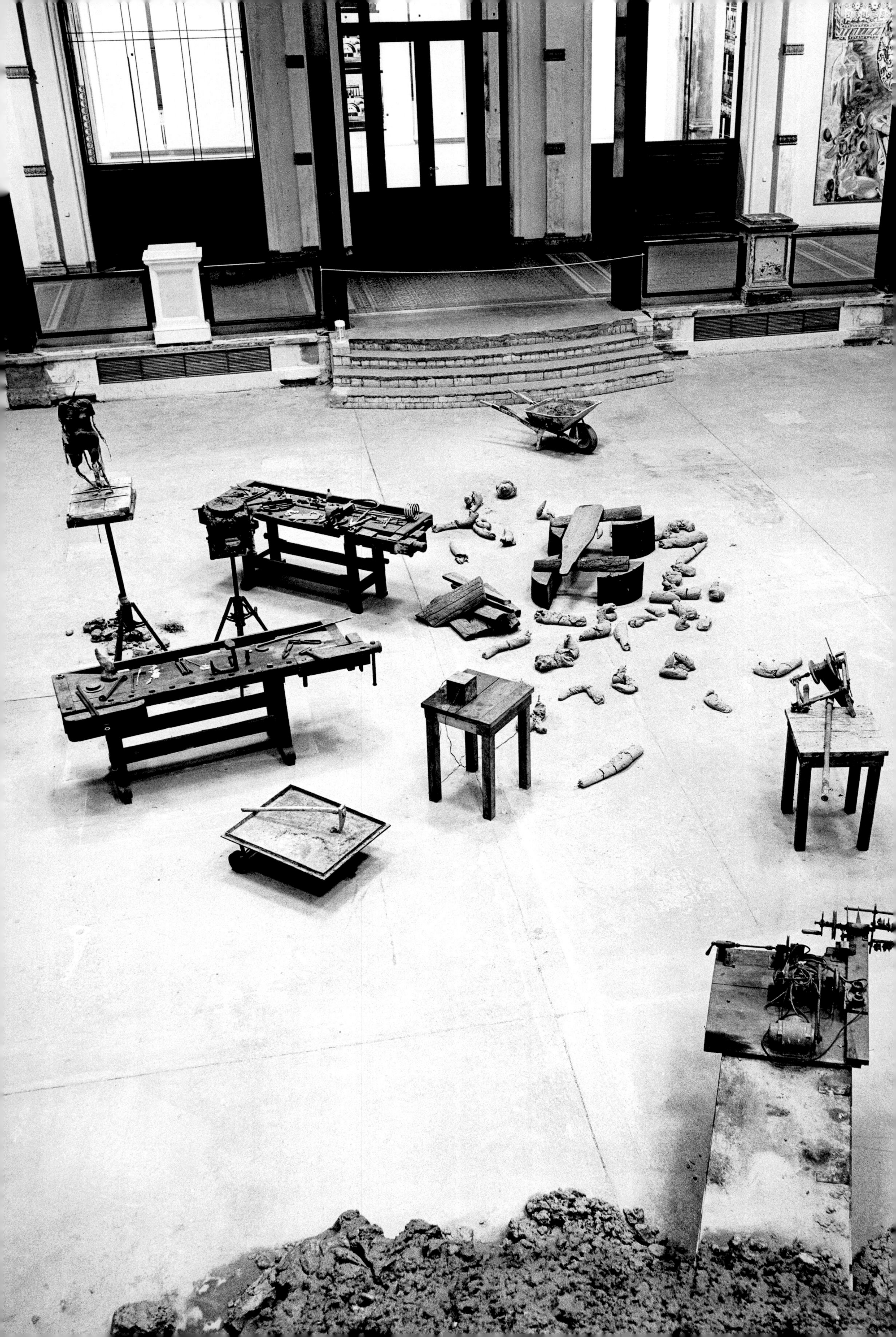

Joseph Beuys, *Zeitgeist*, Martin-Gropius-Bau, Berlin, 1982

Let the last words be given to Beuys, in which he discusses his deliberately democratising multiples:

> [...] art has to do with life. Only from art can a new concept of economics be formed, in terms of human need, not in the sense of use and consumption, politics and property, but above all in terms of the production of spiritual goods. The questions of what shall be produced and how are cultural considerations, and if you think it through are therefore spiritual considerations. That means culture flows through the whole of life right through every detail and its products are the concrete concept of CAPITAL.[17]

Therein lies the true Utopia, achievable alone through Art and the Principle of Hope.

1. Joseph Beuys quoted in *Joseph Beuys: The Multiples, Catalogue Raisonné, Multiples and Prints 1965–80*, eds. Jörg Schellmann and Bernd Klüser, trans. Caroline Tisdall (New York University Press, 1980), unpag.

2. Ibid.

3. The word 'Denkmal' in German can be translated as monument but it also contains the imperative for thinking: 'denken', thus the title also suggests that the sculpture induces a thought process. The connection between sculpture, drawing and thought is essential to Beuys, epitomised in his principle of 'visual thinking'.

4. Joseph Beuys quoted in Bernice Rose, *Joseph Beuys and the Language of Drawing* in *Thinking as Form, The Drawings of Joseph Beuys*, exh. cat., ed. Ann Temkin (Philadelphia Museum of Art and Museum of Modern Art, New York / Thames & Hudson, New York, 1993), p. 91.

5. The exhibition *Scythians: warriors of ancient Siberia* took place at the British Museum from 14 September 2017 to 14 January 2018.

6. Caroline Tisdall, *Joseph Beuys*, exh. cat. (Solomon R. Guggenheim Museum, New York / Thames & Hudson, London, 1979), p. 17.

7. Ibid., p. 9.

8. Ibid., p. 82.

9. Ibid., p. 168.

10. Ibid.

11. Joseph Beuys in *Zeitgeist International Art Exhibition*, exh. cat., eds. Christos M. Joachimides and Norman Rosenthal (Weidenfeld & Nicholson, London, 1983), p. 82. See also pp. 31–33.

12. Ibid.

13. Ernst Bloch, *The Principle of Hope* (MIT Press, Cambridge, Massachusetts, 1986), vol. 1, p. 3.

14. Ibid., p. 219.

15. Ibid., p. 282.

16. Ibid., p. 1199.

17. *Joseph Beuys: The Multiples*, eds. Jörg Schellmann and Bernd Klüser, unpag.

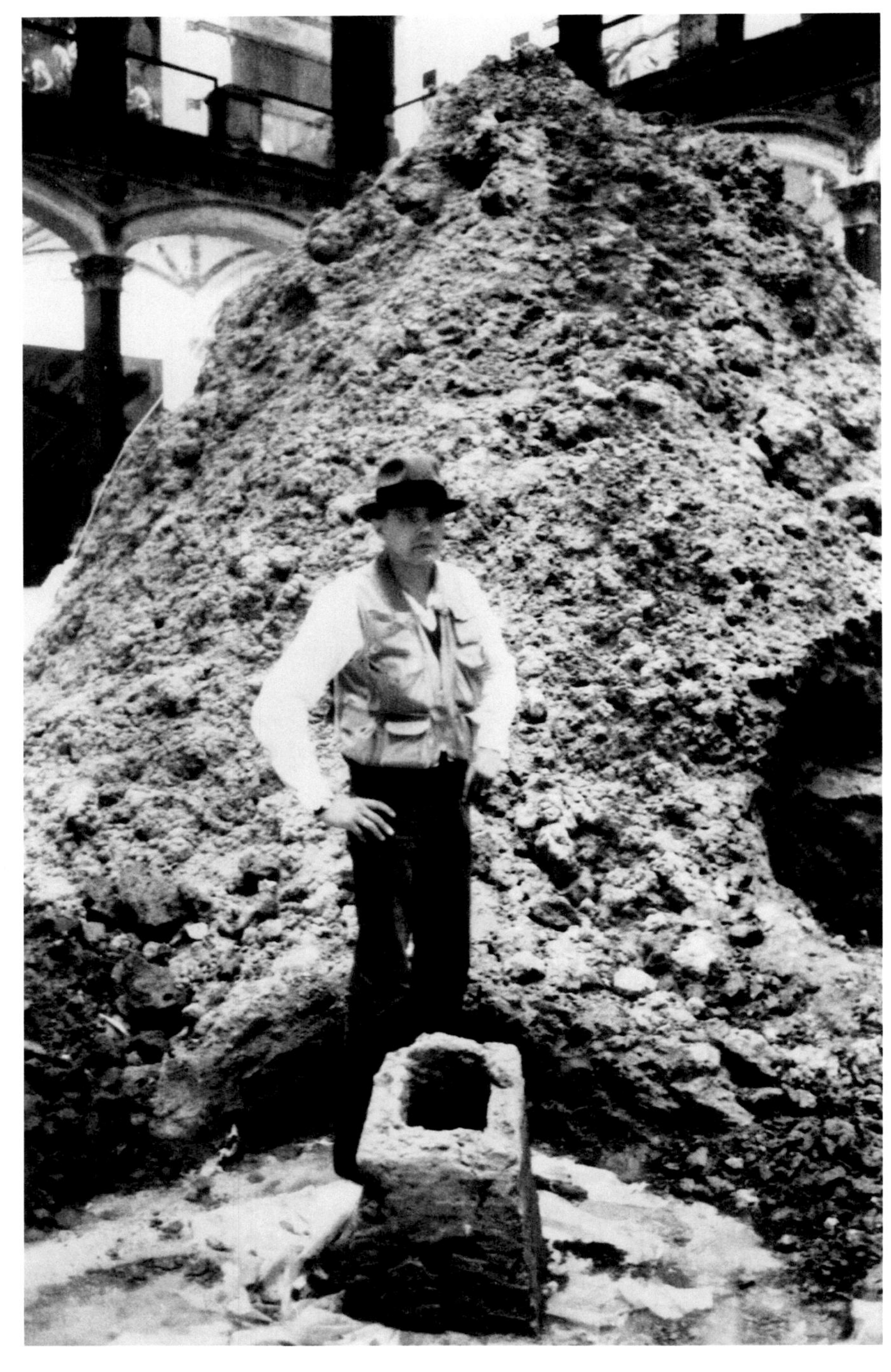

Joseph Beuys with *Lehmofen* [Clay Oven]
at Martin-Gropius-Bau, Berlin, 1983

JOSEPH BEUYS

+ – WURST
(jetzt geht es um die Wurst)
" " " " **DAS GANZE**

Ich würde nicht von mir behaupten, daß ich nicht dumm bin, „denn daß es um die radikale Um-**GESTALTUNG DES GANZEN** geht, das weiß im Grunde gerade der Dümmste. Er sagt sich im Stillen: die Intelligenz, die benötigt wird eine **BLUTWURST** zu machen – das kann ja nur die Intelligenz der Blutwurst selbst sein."

LEHM
WERKSTATT
Die Hirschdenkmäler sind Akkumulationsmaschinen an denen Menschen und alle anderen Geister sich treffen, um gemeinsam zu arbeiten und dabei die entscheidenden Gesichtspunkte zu besprechen, die nötig sind den **KAPITALBEGRIFF** und damit die Weltlage in die richtige **FORM** zu bringen. Das kann man natürlich ohne Hirschdenkmäler nicht.
Lehm ist Stoff der Erde, Ton und Kiesel. Mit einem rechten Bestandteil von Kalk haben wir den Untergrund auf dem wir stehn und aus dem wir den Planeten nach den furchtbaren Vertotungen wieder zum Leben erwecken werden.
Ich behaupte, daß dieser Begriff **SOZIALE PLASTIK** eine völlig neue Kategorie der Kunst ist. Eine neue Muse tritt den alten Musen gegenüber auf! Diese Muse war vorher gar nicht bekannt, und weil sie nicht bekannt war, ist es zu den bekannten Denkirrtümern gekommen, d. h. jetzt ist die Lage so kritisch geworden, daß sich wirklich einige Geister auf den Weg gemacht haben diese Muse zu entdecken. Sie trägt den zukünftigen Begriff von Plastik der vor jedem anderen Begriff von Plastik Vorrang hat. Ich schreie sogar: es wird keine brauchbare Plastik mehr hienieden geben, wenn dieser **SOZIALE ORGANISMUS ALS LEBEWESEN** nicht da ist. Das ist die Idee des Gesamtkunstwerkes in dem **JEDER MENSCH EIN KÜNSTLER** ist.
Die Hirschdenkmäler sind in sich ein Ding, vielleicht sogar ein sehr simples Ding. Aber sie sind doch auch ein Zeichen dafür, daß jetzt viel, viel mehr Akteure **BEI DIESER AUSEINANDERSETZUNG** da sein werden. Da steht der Hirsch, und der Hirsch ist ja kein Mensch. Er ist für das gewöhnliche Bewußtsein ein Bestandteil der Natur. Aber wie regiert nun die Natur mit, wenn jede zukünftige Natur eine von Menschen gemachte Natur sein wird? Natur wird . . . nicht Kultur! Dieses Wort können wir schon nicht mehr hören, nachdem es so zur Kulturschande gemacht worden ist in der Bundesrepublik Deutschland und auch anderswo. Nicht Kultur aber Wirtschaftsleben, das den erweiterten Kunstbegriff und damit das Freiheitswesen in sich aufgenommen hat. Kunst als Integral des Wirtschaftslebens. So sind wir denn zuhause.
Das Hirschdenkmal ist ein Zeichen für den vom Menschen geschaffenen Geist in der Natur, der Maschinen bewegt. (Beweis für die Realität der Idee und für die Falschheit der Entropielehre.) Vernichtete oder ausgestorbene Tiere und vernichtete oder ausgestorbene Menschen treffen sich an den Maschinen. Sie sind ja in der Wirklichkeit, auch wenn sie ausgestorben sind, denn sie treiben die Maschinen an, da an der Berliner Mauer.
Ja, nun kurz und gut, wenn man das in Worten ausdrücken könnte auf einfache Art, dann brauchte man die Blutwürste nicht zu machen.

Text by Joseph Beuys originally published in *Zeitgeist: internationale Kunstausstellung Berlin* Martin Gropius Bau, exh. cat., eds. Christos M. Joachimides and Norman Rosenthal (Frölich & Kaufmann, Berlin, 1982)

JOSEPH BEUYS

+ – 'WURST' or BLOOD PUDDING
(the blood's up: it's ALL or nothing)

I would not say of myself that I am not stupid, 'for at heart it's just the most stupid who know that what is at stake is the radical **TRANS-FORMATION OF ALL, OF THE WHOLE.** Quietly, he says to himself: the intelligence needed to make a **BLOOD PUDDING** – that can only be the intelligence of the blood pudding itself.'

CLAY
WORKSHOP
The stag monuments are accumulation machines at which human beings and all other spirits meet, in order to work together and in so doing to discuss every decisive point of view necessary for putting the **CONCEPT OF CAPITAL** and with that the situation of the world into the proper **FORM.** That cannot of course be done without stag monuments. Clay is a substance of the earth, clay and quartz. With a proper part of chalk we have the subsoil on which we stand and out of which after the terrible making-dead we will re-awaken the planet to life. I claim that this concept of **SOCIAL SCULPTURE** is a completely new category of art. A new muse appears opposite the old muses! Before, this muse was not known at all,

and because she was not known, she has joined the known mistakes in thinking, i.e. now the situation has become so critical that a number of spirits have set out to discover the new muse. She contains the future concept of sculpture which has priority over every other concept of sculpture. I even scream: there will no longer be any useful sculpture down here if this **SOCIAL ORGANISM AS A LIVING BEING** is not also here. That is the idea of the 'Gesamtkunstwerk' in which **EVERY HUMAN BEING IS AN ARTIST.** The stag monuments are really a thing, perhaps even a very simple thing. But they are also a sign for the fact that many, many more actors will be present **AT THIS DEBATE.** There stands the stag, and a stag is not, after all, a human being. For the normal cast of mind he is a part of nature. But how will nature join in government if all future nature is a nature made by people? Nature will ... not be culture! We can't stand the word culture any more, since it has been turned into a cultural scandal in the Federal Republic of Germany and elsewhere as well. Not culture but economic life, which has come to include the extended concept of art and with that the essence of freedom. Art as integral to economic life. So now we're back home again. The stag monument is a sign for that man-made spirit in nature which drives machines. (Proof that the Idea is real and that the theory of entropy is false.) Annihilated or extinct animals meet annihilated or extinct peoples by the machines. For they are in reality, even if they have died out, because they're driving the machines, here at the Berlin wall. Yes, in a word, if you could say it in words in a simple way, you wouldn't have to make blood pudding. Adapted by Jeremy Adler

COMPENDIUM

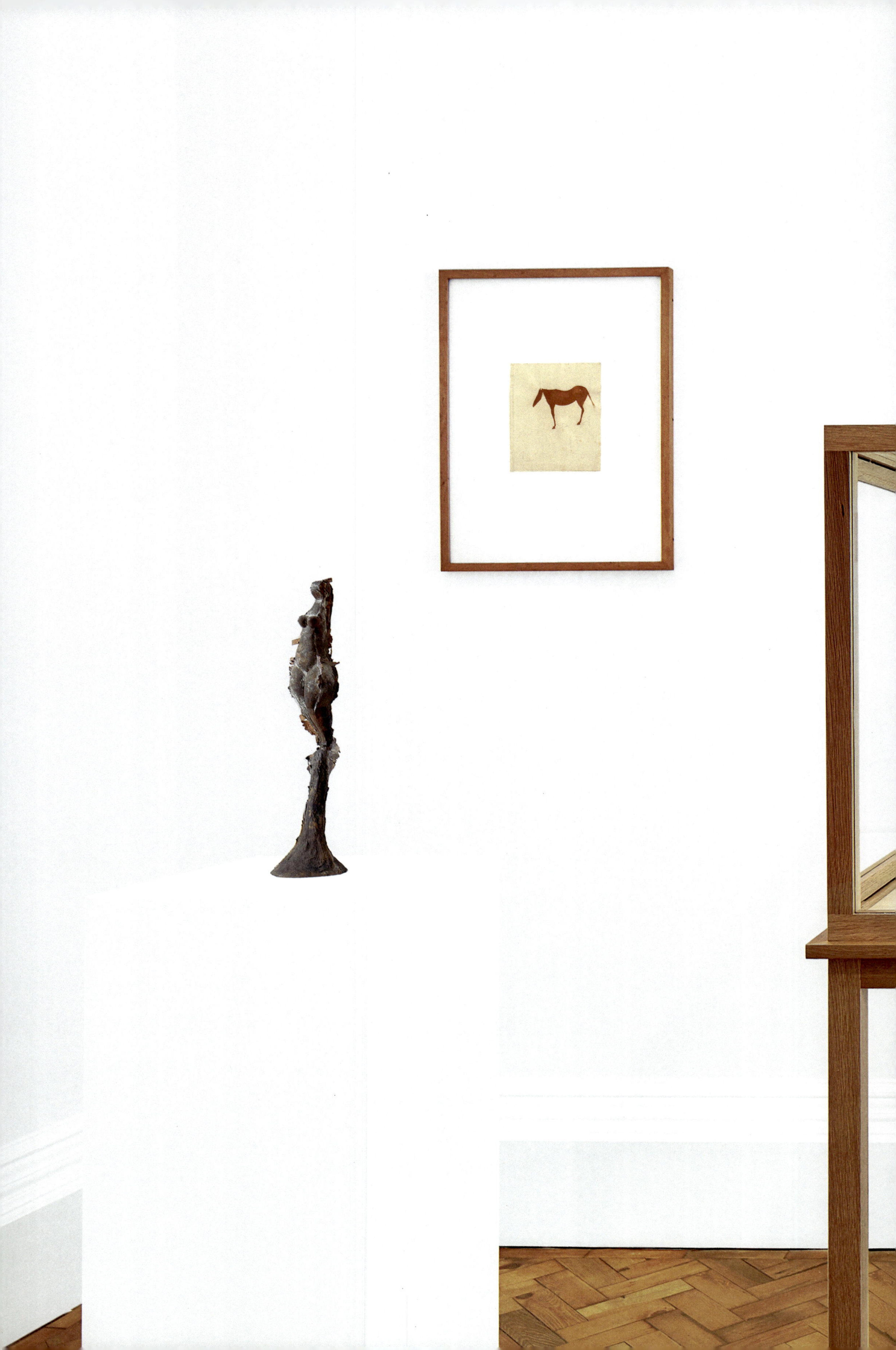

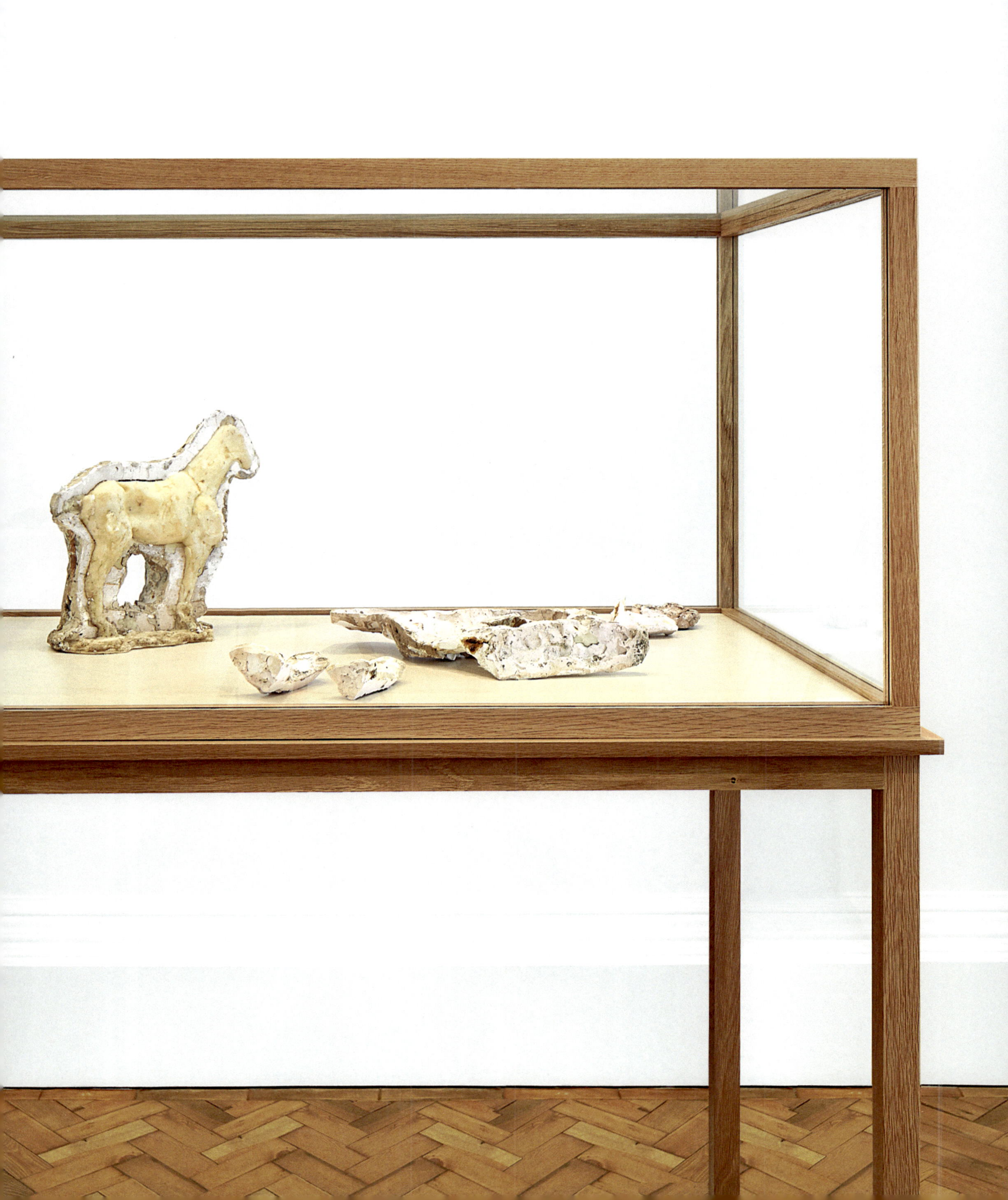

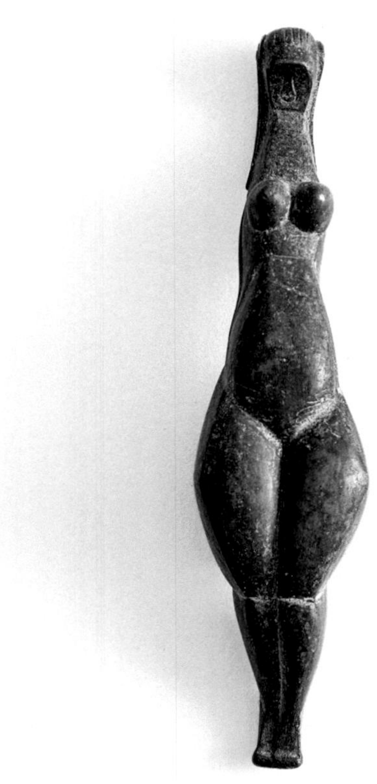

Bleifrau [Lead Woman], 1949
Lead cast (front and side)
6 x 22.6 x 6 cm (2.36 x 8.89 x 2.36 in)

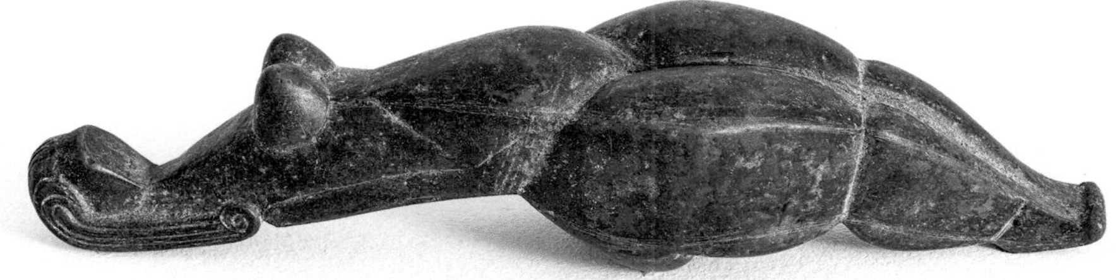

Tierfrau [Animal Woman], 1949 (cast 1979)
Bronze
46.7 x 13.3 x 10 cm (18.39 x 5.24 x 3.94 in)

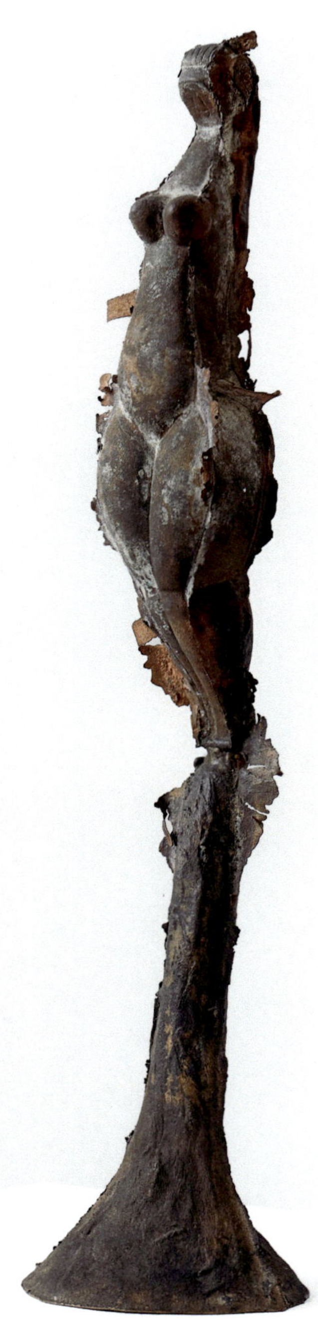

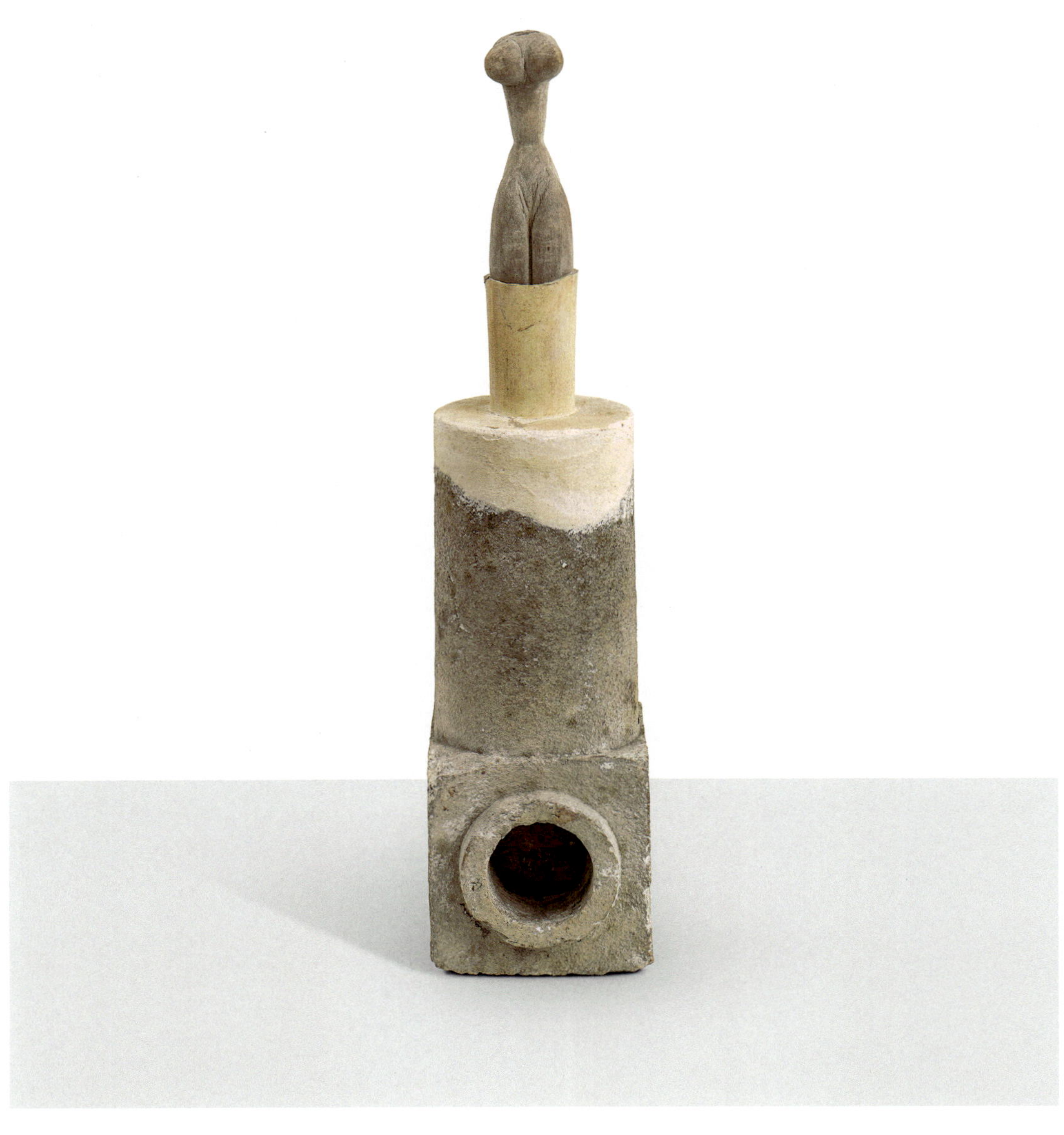

Ofen (1950) *mit Torso* (1948)
[Oven (1950) with Torso (1948)], 1948–50
Wood, cardboard, plaster, concrete
31 x 7.2 x 8.3 cm (12.2 x 2.83 x 3.27 in)

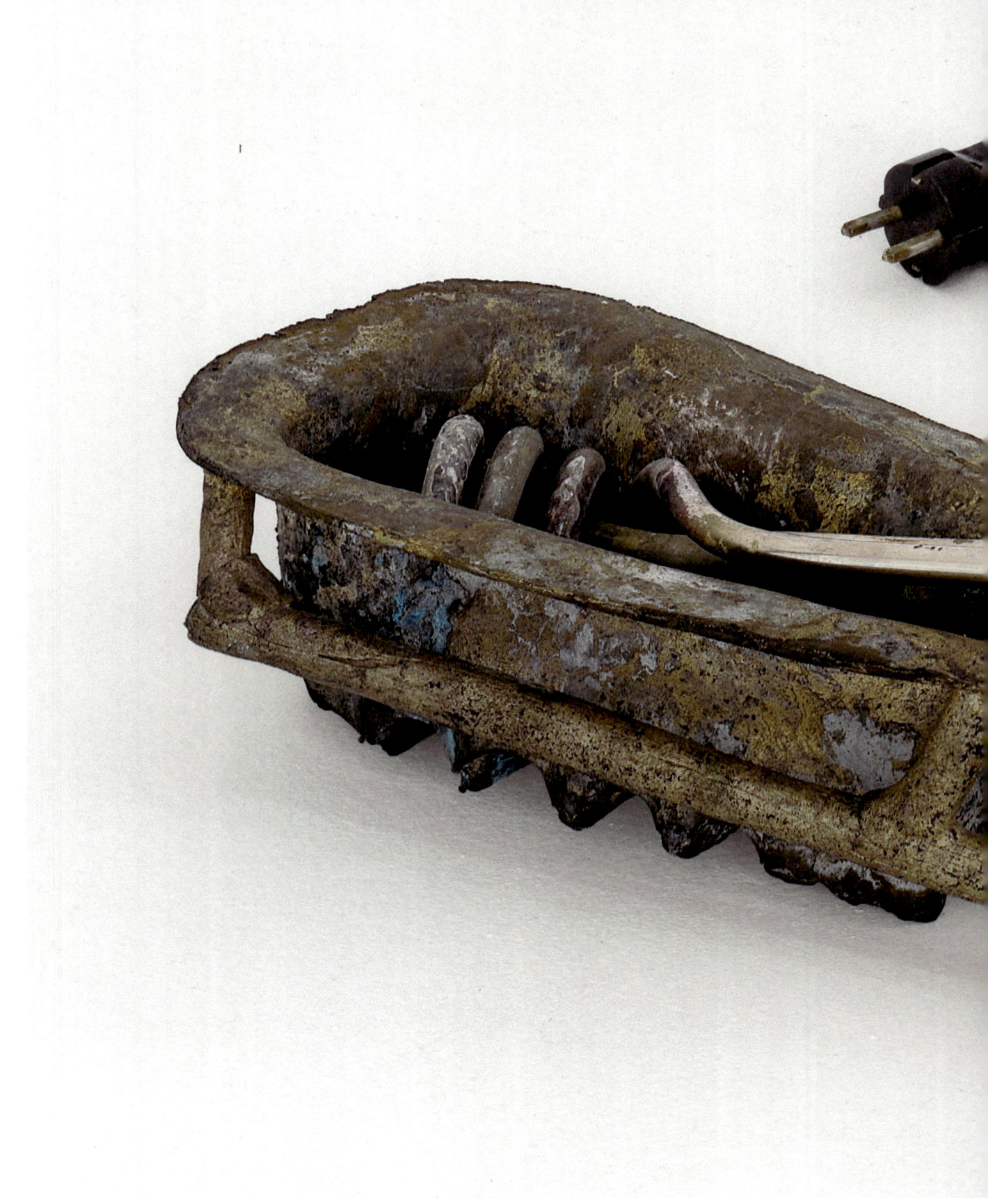

Badewanne für eine Heldin
[Bathtub for a Heroine], 1950/1961/1984
Bronze, immersion heater with lead
Oven: 31 x 7 x 7.5 cm (12.2 x 2.76 x 2.95 in)
Bathtub: 23 x 14 x 9.5 cm (9.06 x 5.51 x 3.74 in)

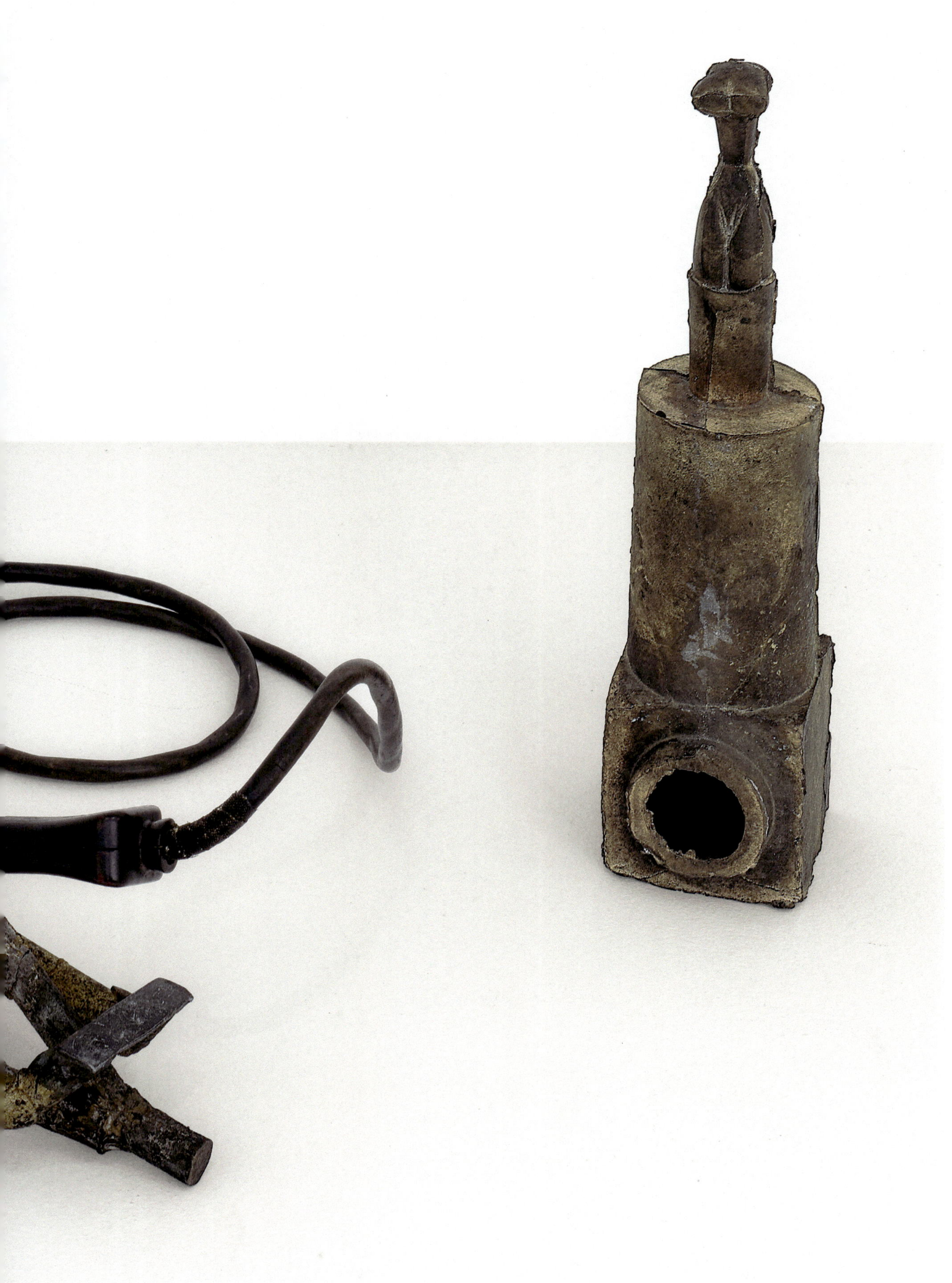

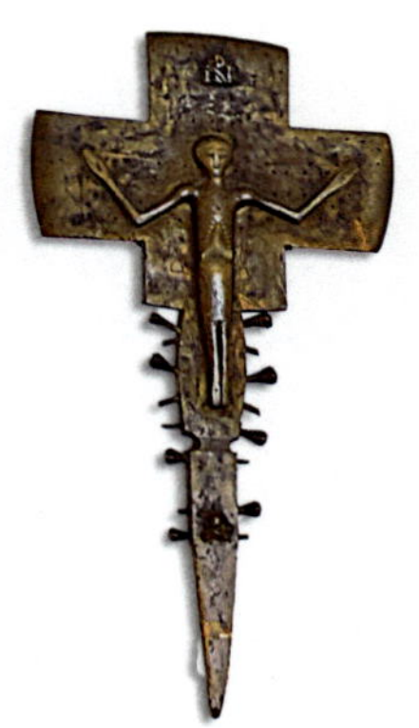

Kreuze [Crosses], 1949–53

Tierfrau [Animal Woman], 1949 (cast 1979)

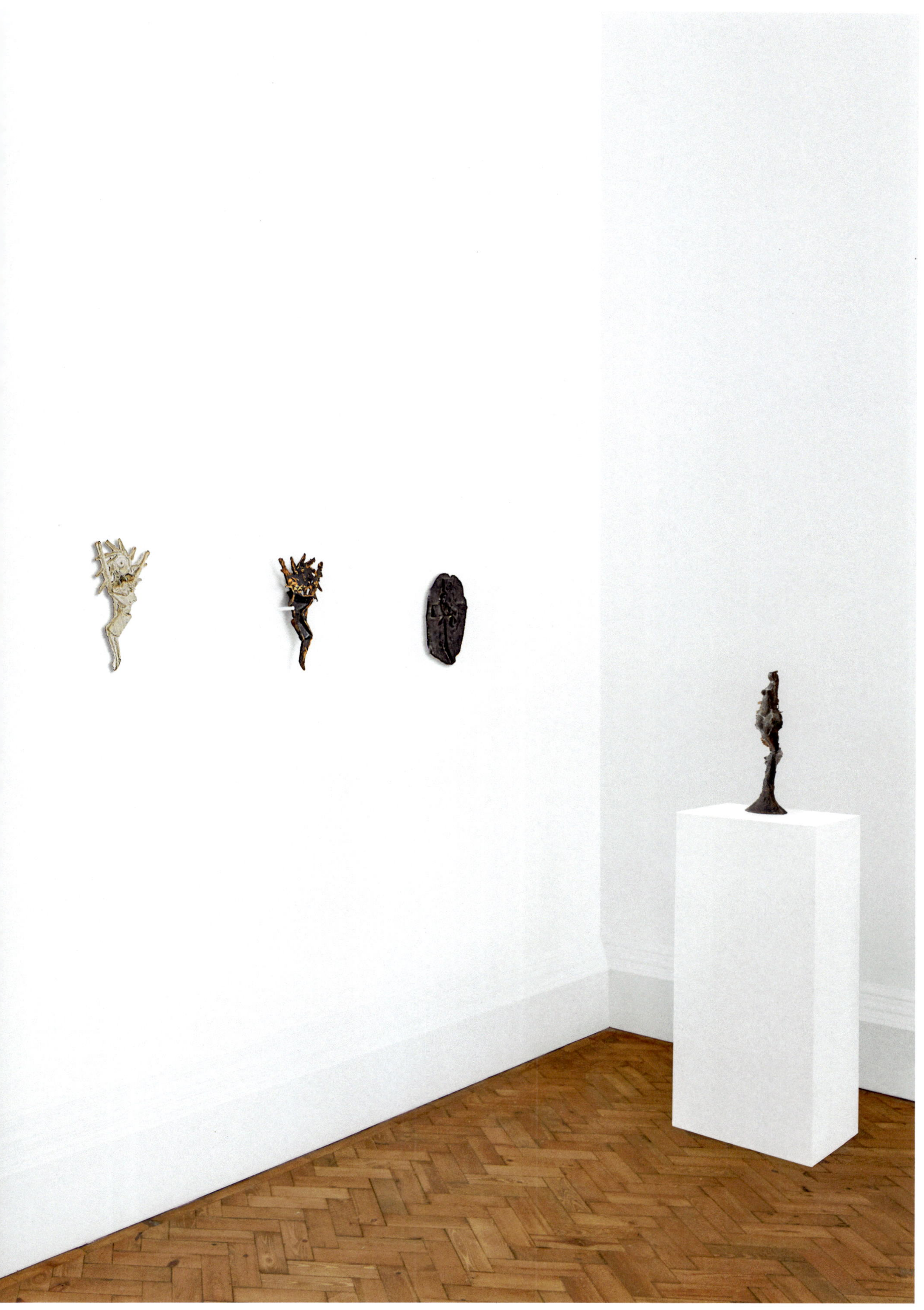

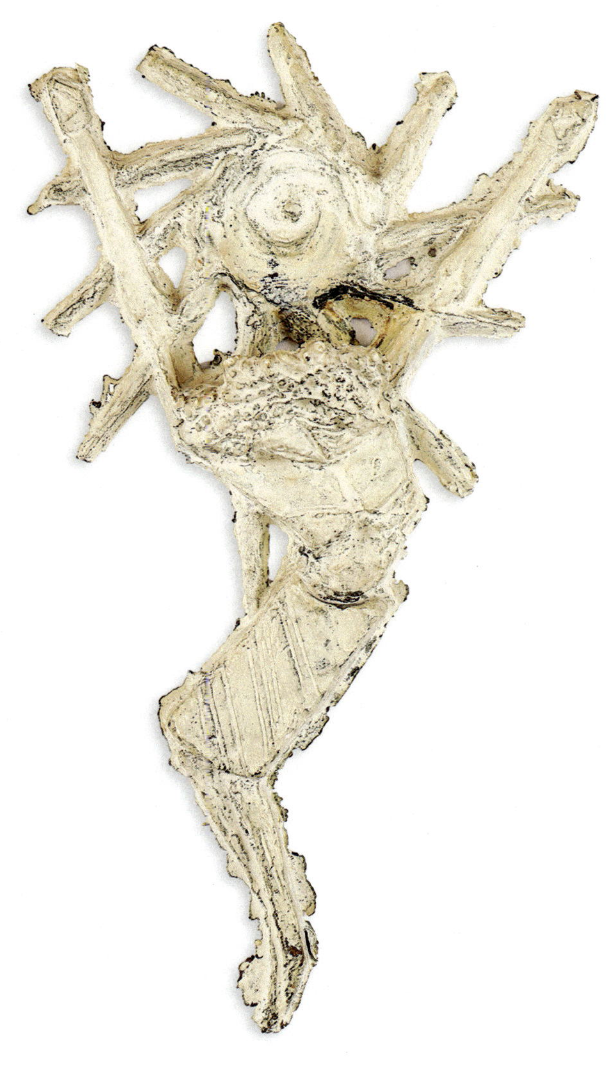

Gekreuzigter Christus (mit Sonne)
MODELL VERSUCH I
[Crucified Christ (with Sun)
MODEL ATTEMPT I], 1949
White painted bronze
36 x 20.4 x 4.6 cm (14.17 x 8.03 x 1.81 in)

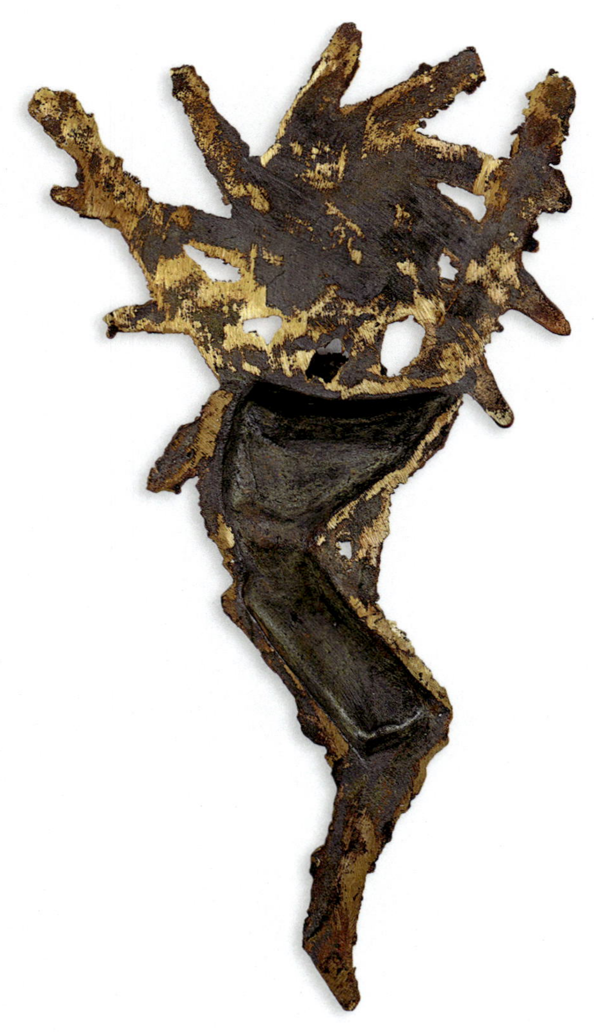

Gekreuzigter Christus (mit Sonne)
[Crucified Christ (with Sun)], 1949
Bronze (back and front)
35.7 x 19.8 x 4.5 cm (14.06 x 7.8 x 1.77 in)

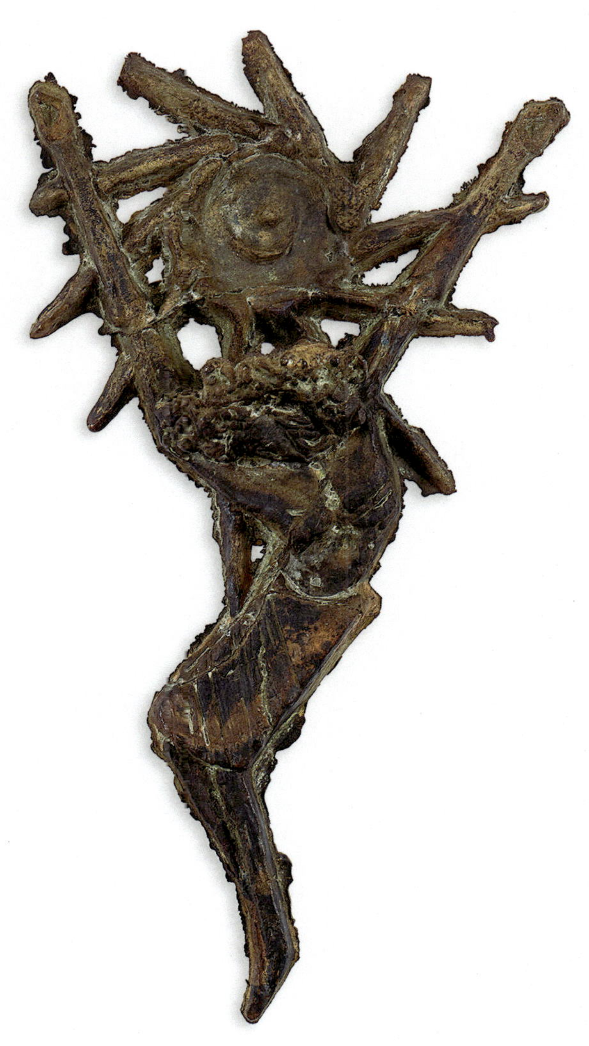

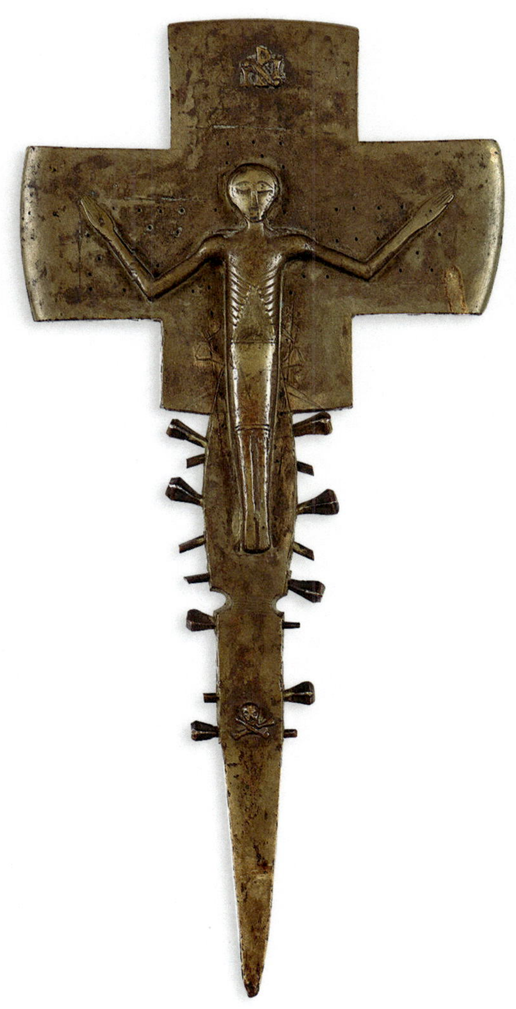

1 Kreuz [1 Cross], undated (before 1953)
Brass cast
46 x 23 x 2 cm (18.11 x 9.06 x 0.79 in)

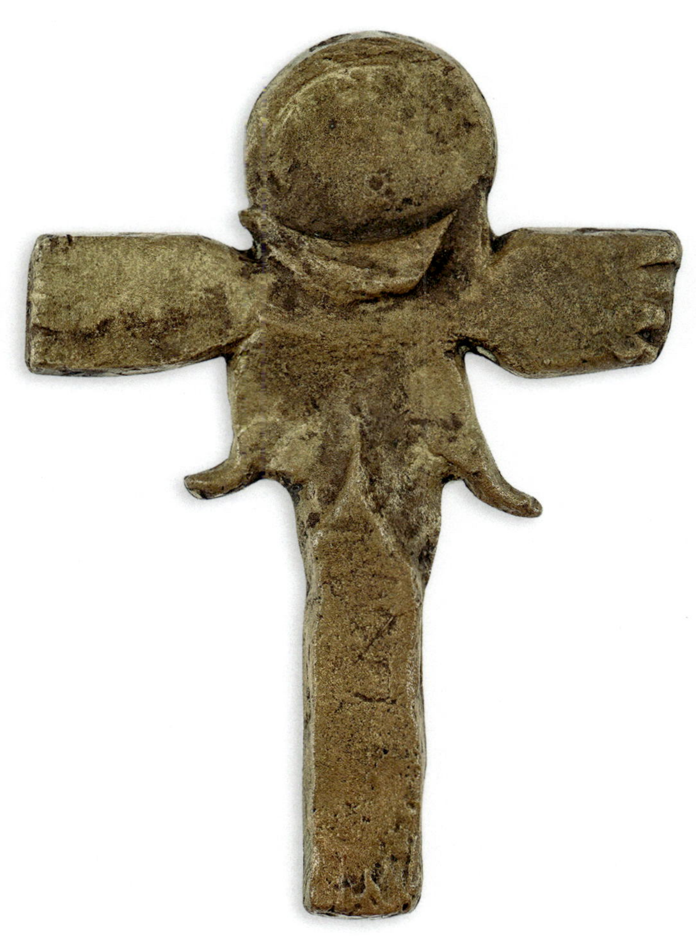

Kleines Kreuz [Small Cross], 1949
Bronze
17.4 x 12.9 x 1 cm (6.85 x 5.08 x 0.39 in)

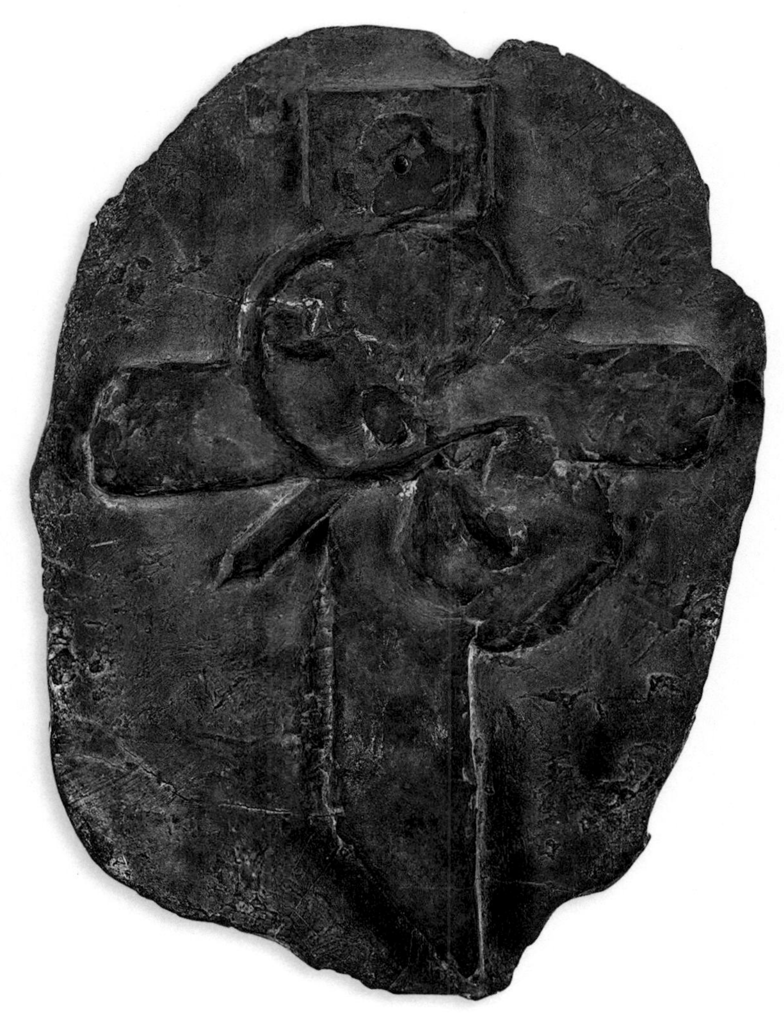

Wurfkreuz [Throwing Cross], 1951
Bronze
33 x 24 x 1.8 cm
(13 x 9.45 x 0.71 in)

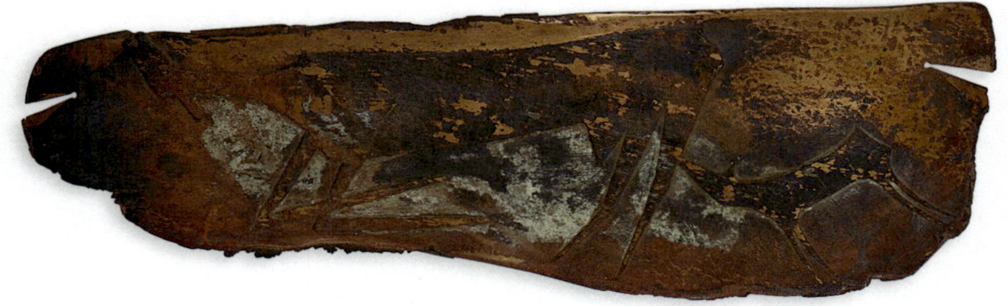

Hirschkuh mit Jungem [Doe with Calf], 1948
Bronze
17.2 x 56.8 x 1.2 cm
(6.77 x 22.36 x 0.47 in)

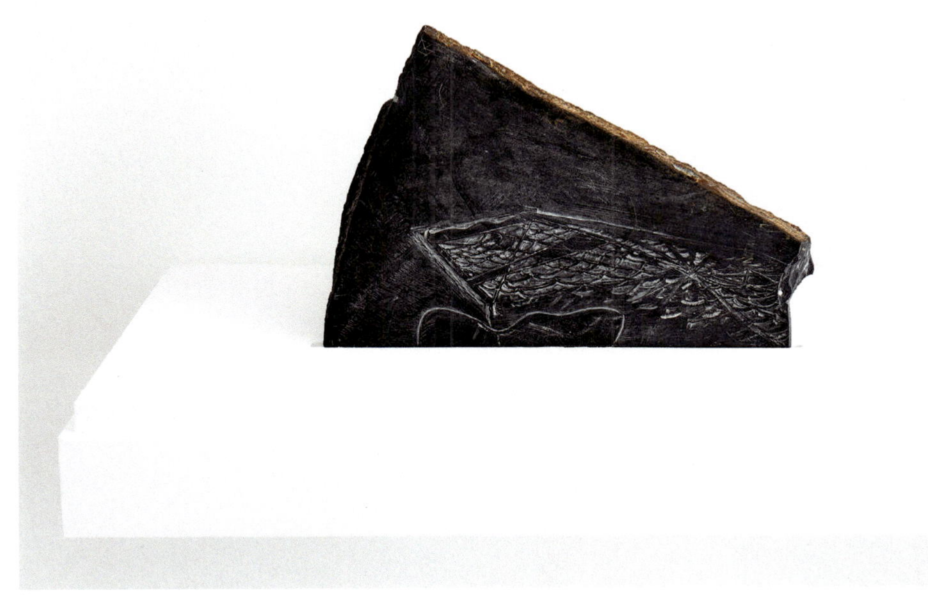

Das Wattenmeer [The Wadden Sea], 1949–50
Carved slate
15 x 21 cm (5.91 x 8.27 in)

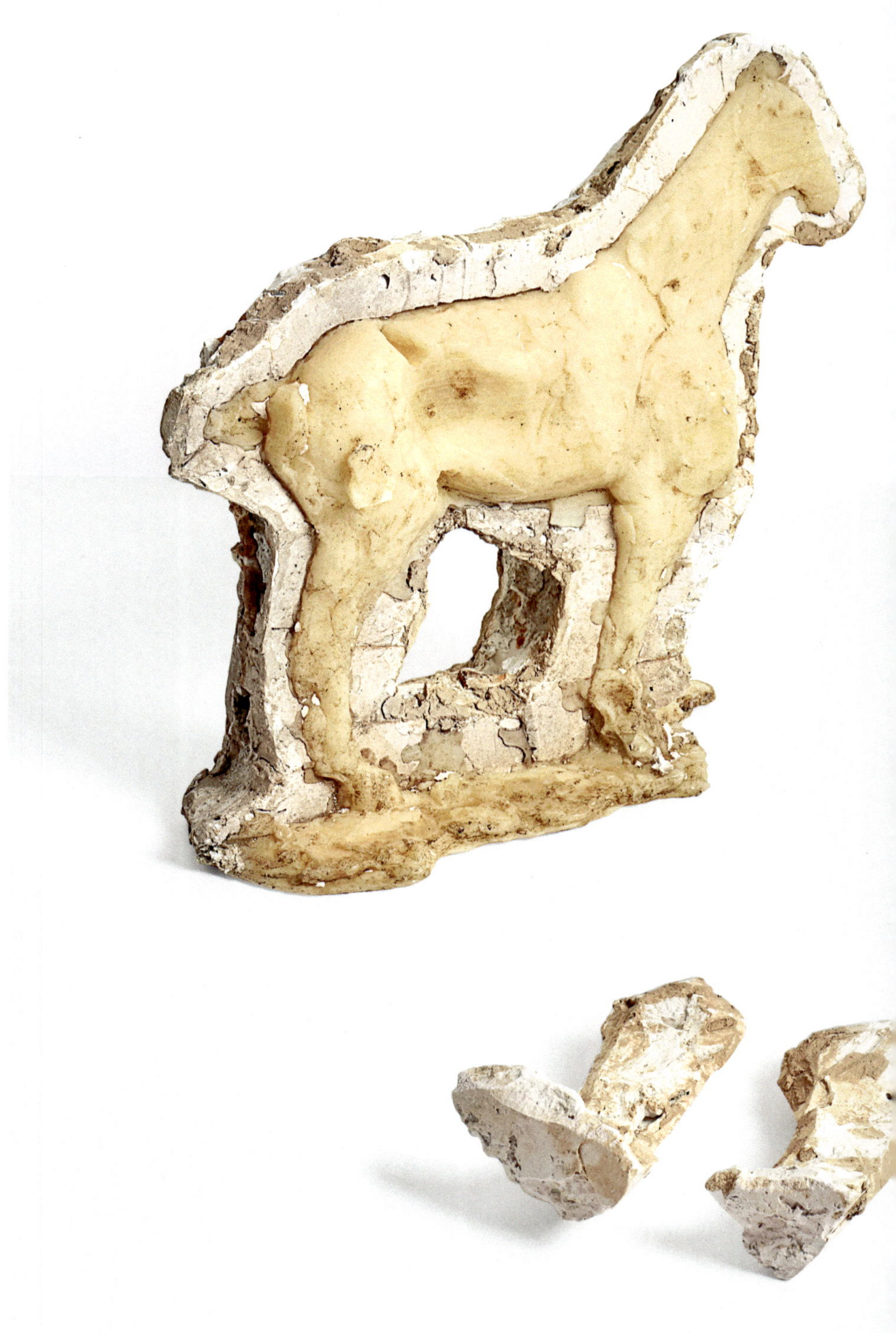

Junges Pferdchen [Young Horse], 1955–86
Wax cast
Installed (approx.): 28.5 x 120 x 81.5 cm
(11.22 x 47.24 x 32.09 in)

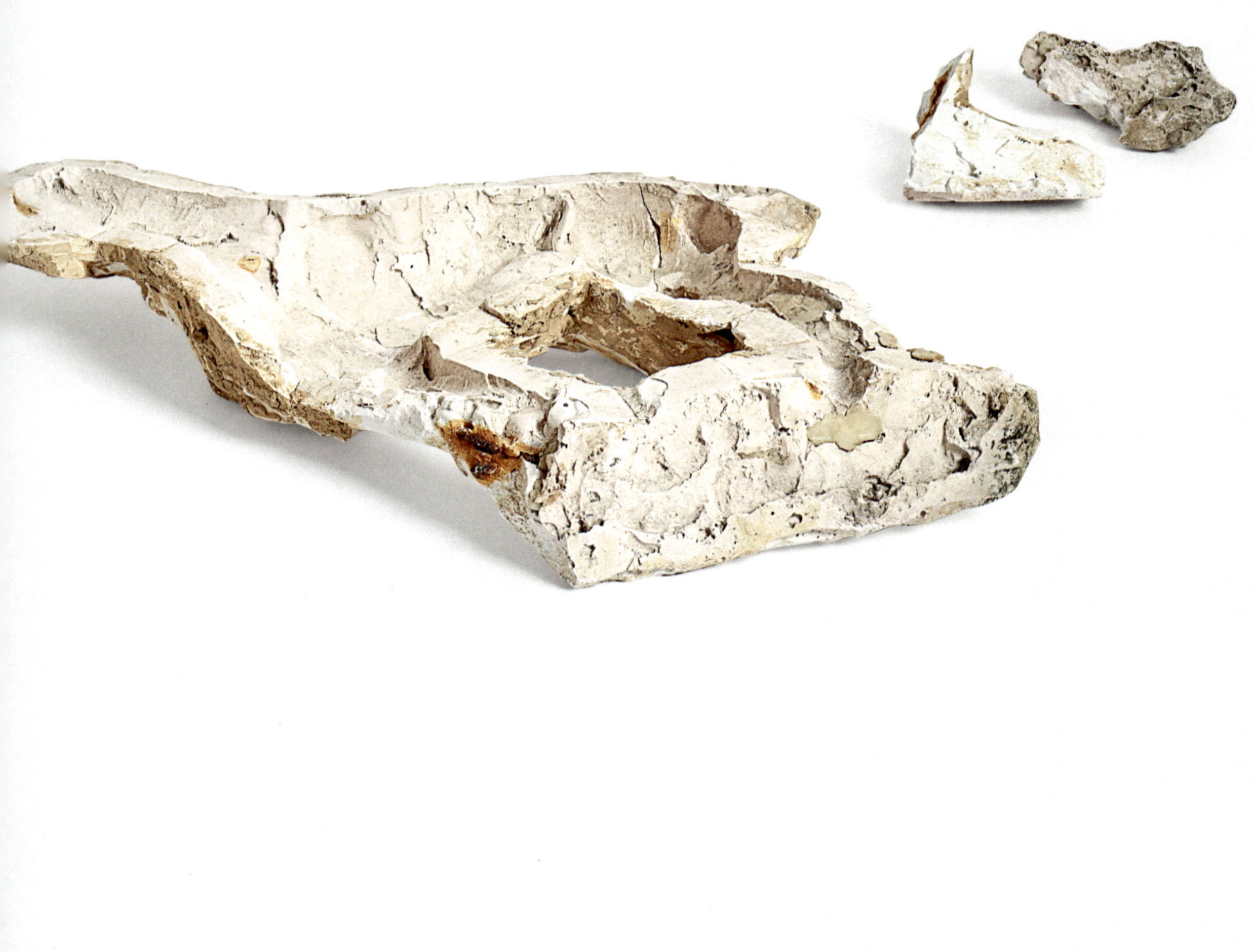

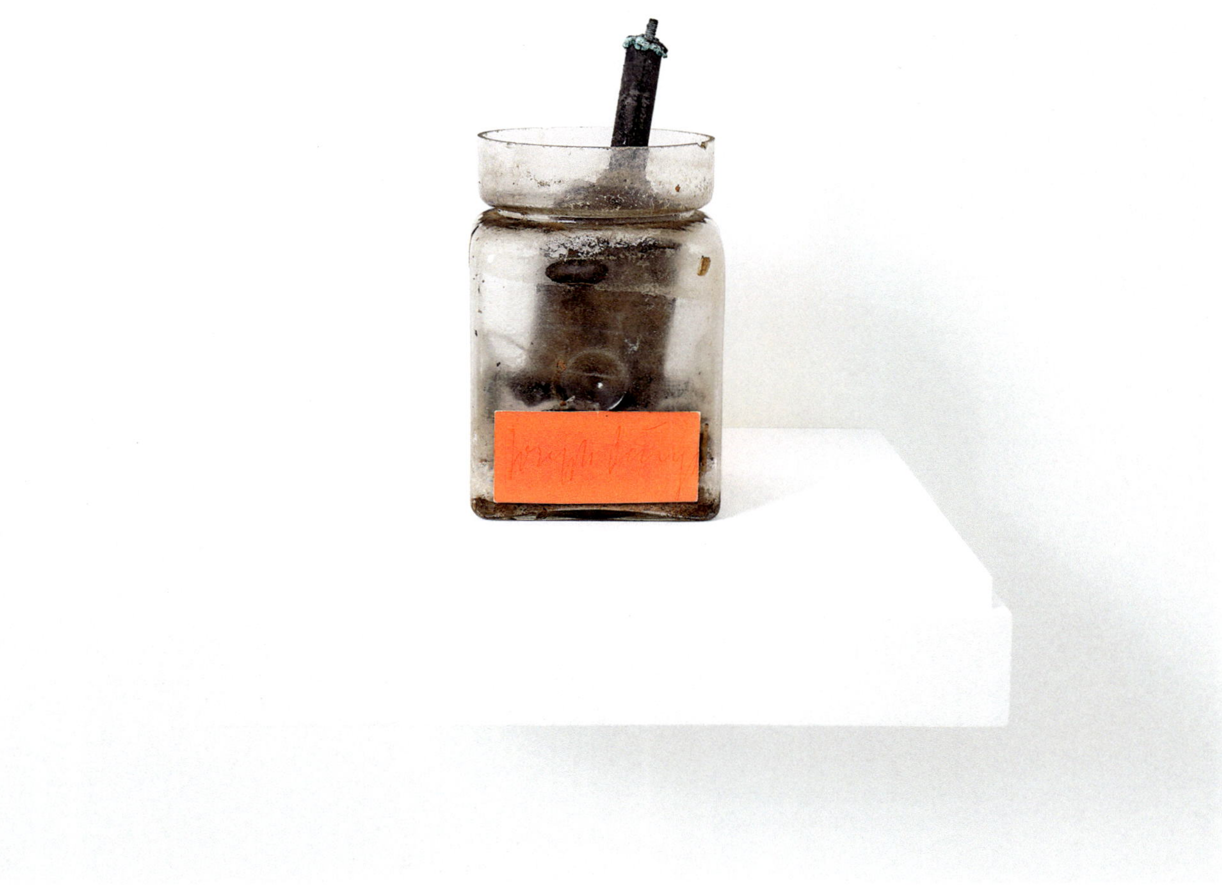

Naßbatterie [Wet Battery], 1973–74
Mixed media with glass, crystals and battery
23.1 x 9.9 x 9.9 cm (9.1 x 3.9 x 3.9 in)

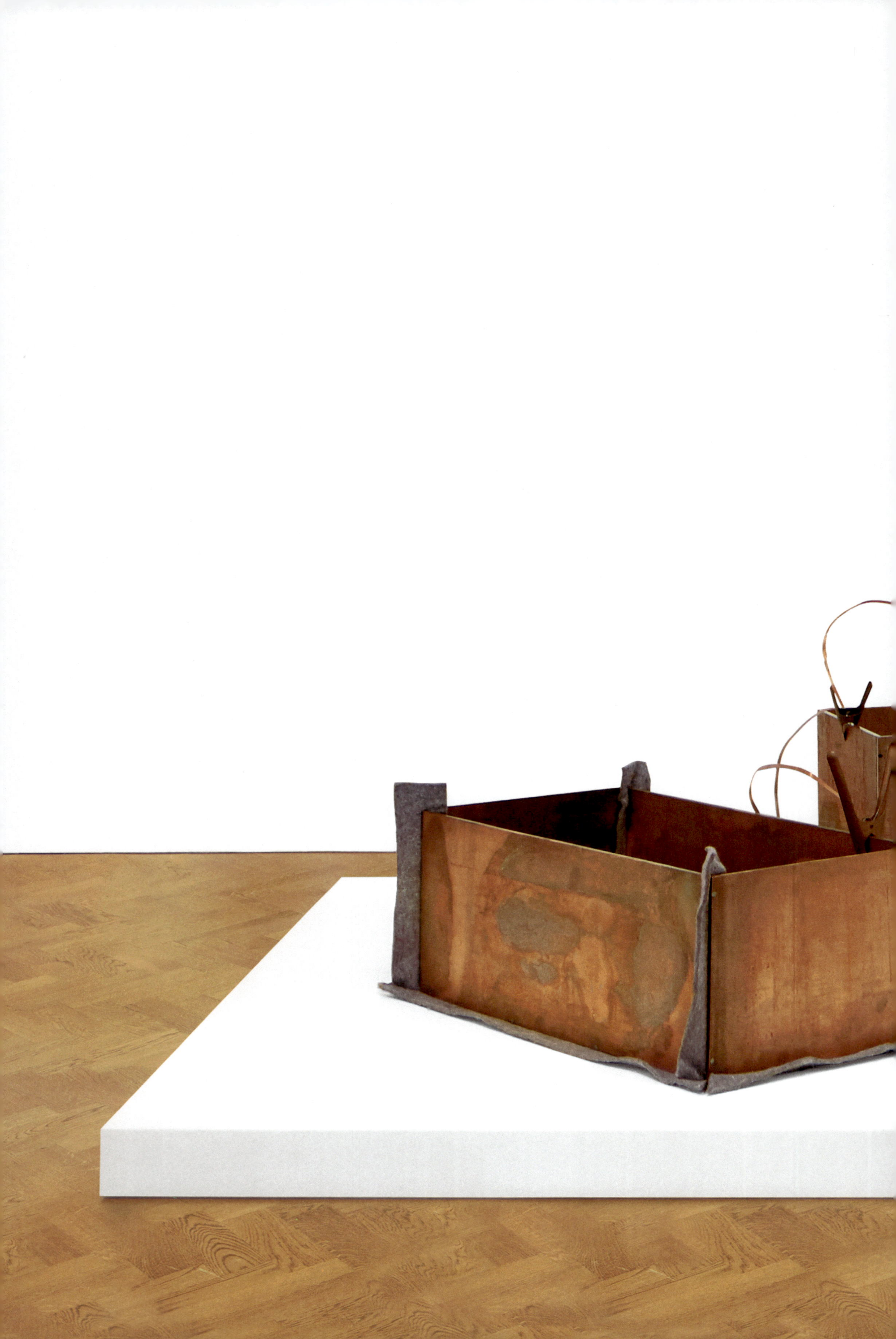

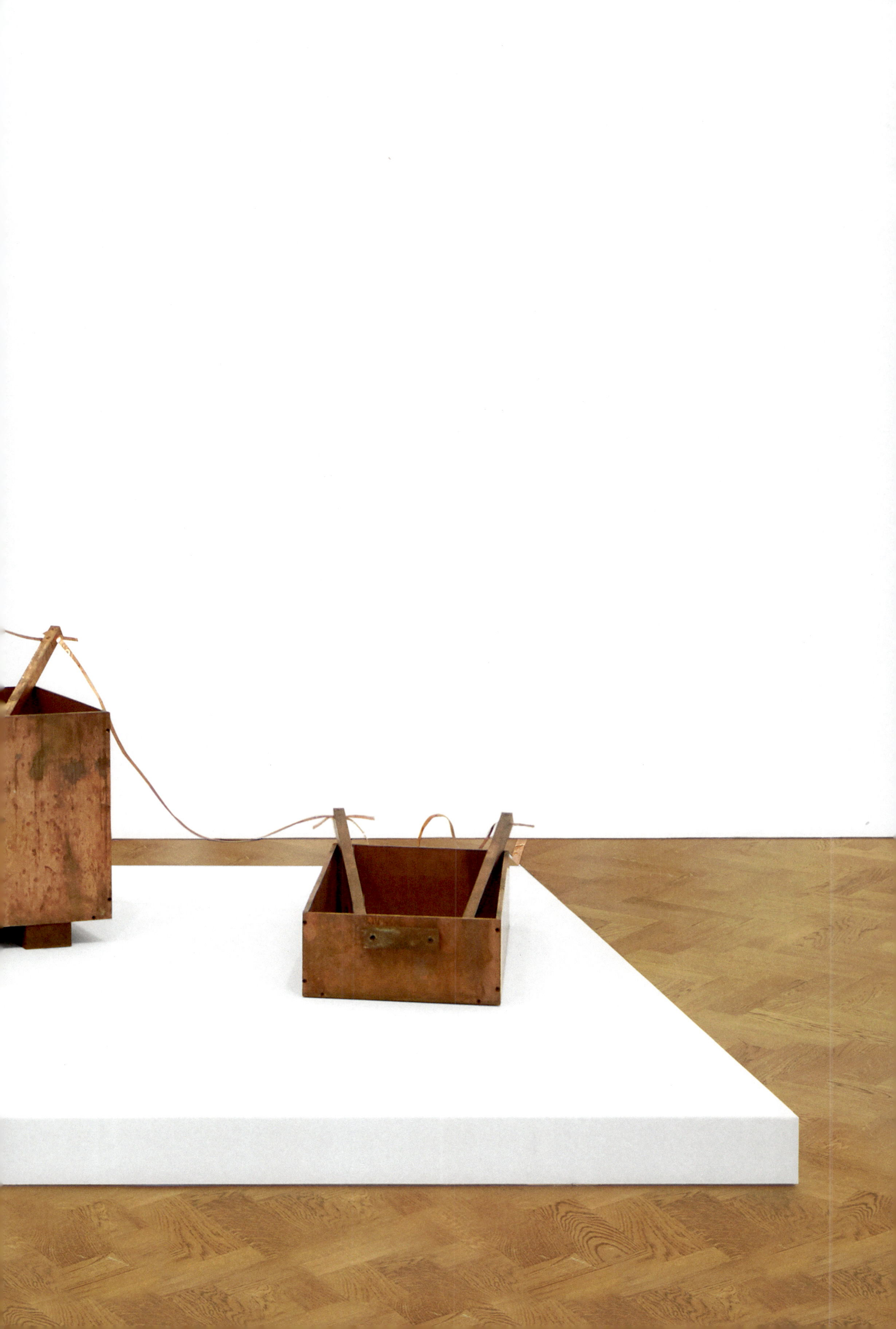

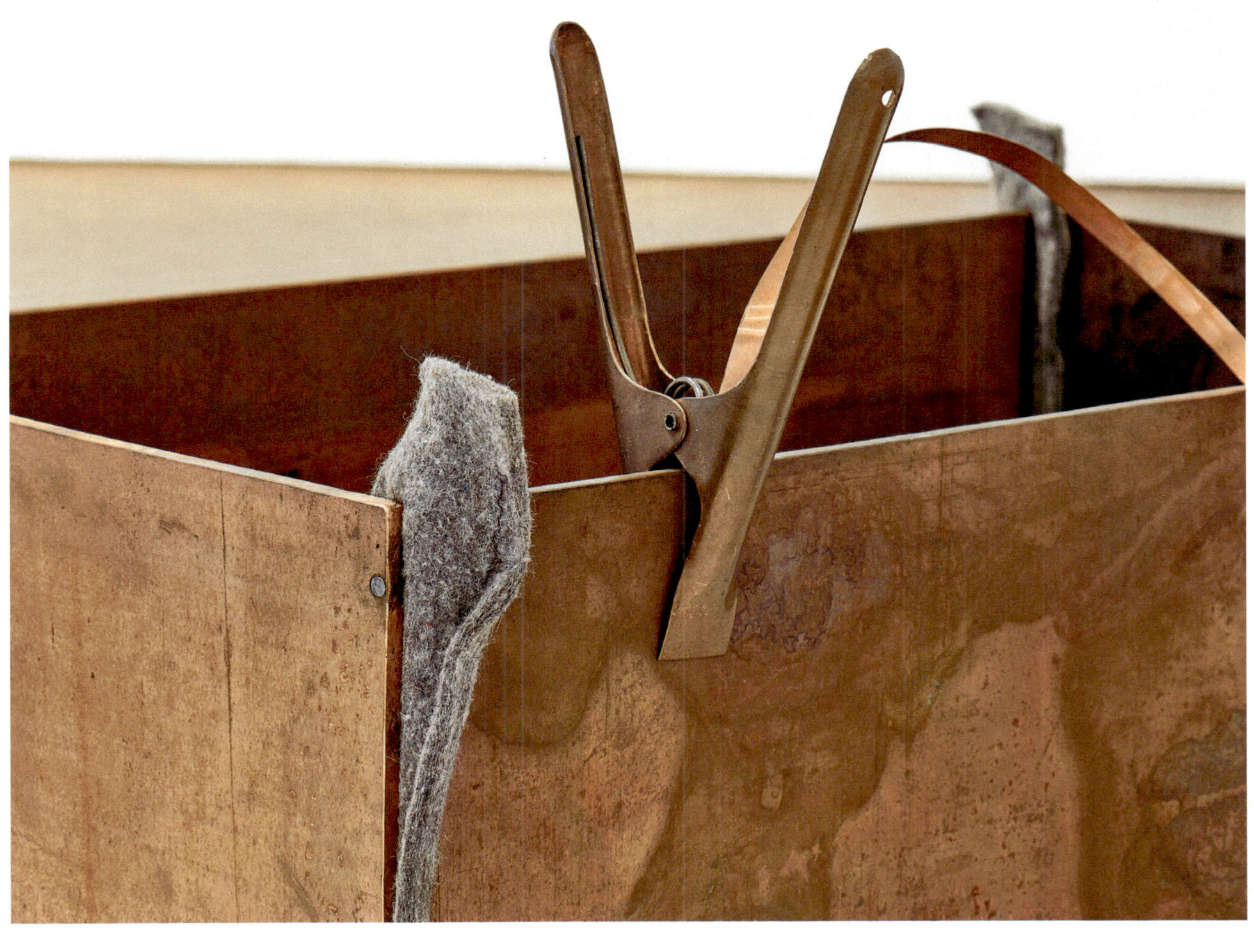

Pages 64–69
Kleines Kraftwerk [Small Power Station], 1984
Copper, iron and felt
Installed: 50.5 x 200 x 150 cm
(19.88 x 78.74 x 59.06 in)

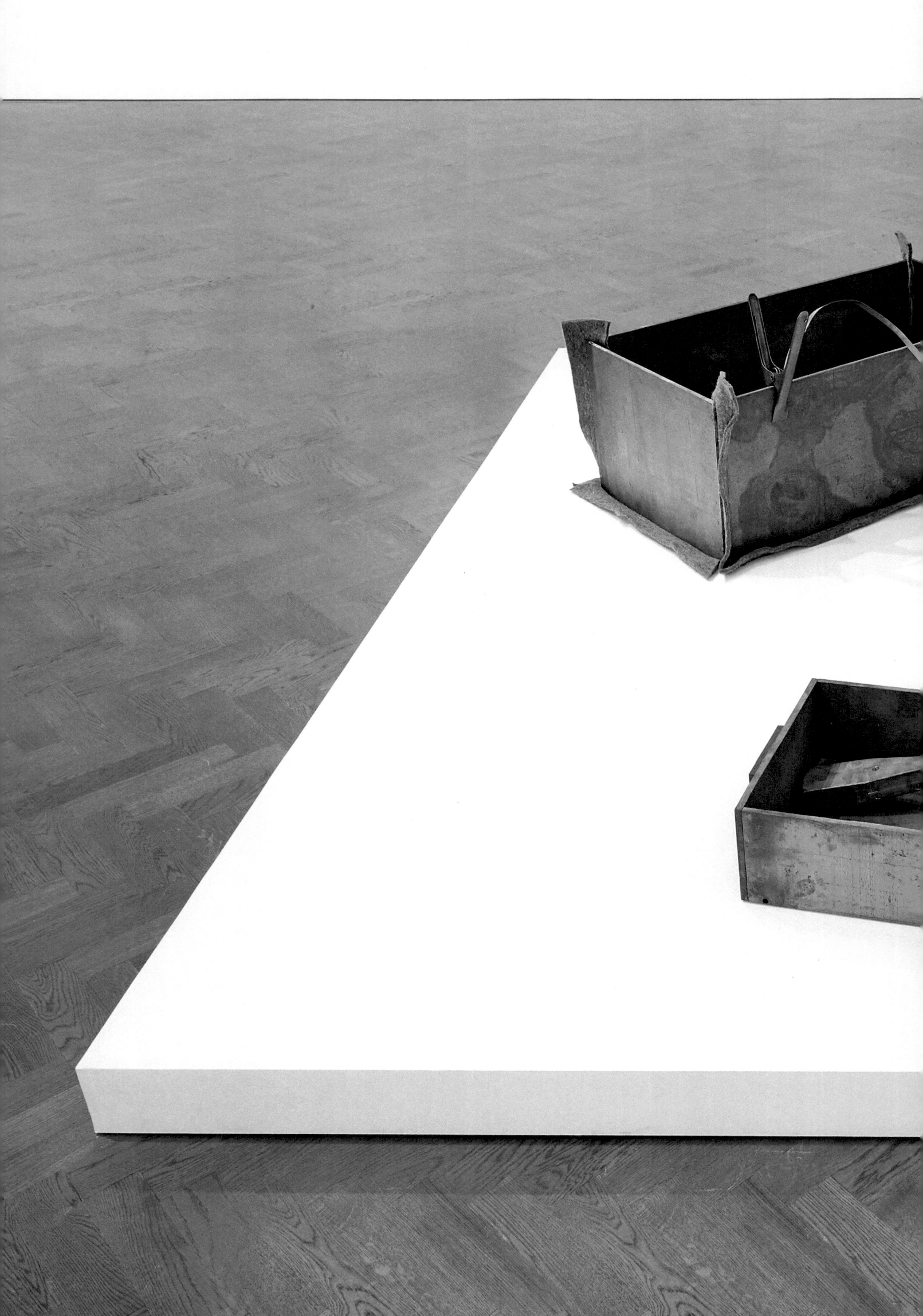

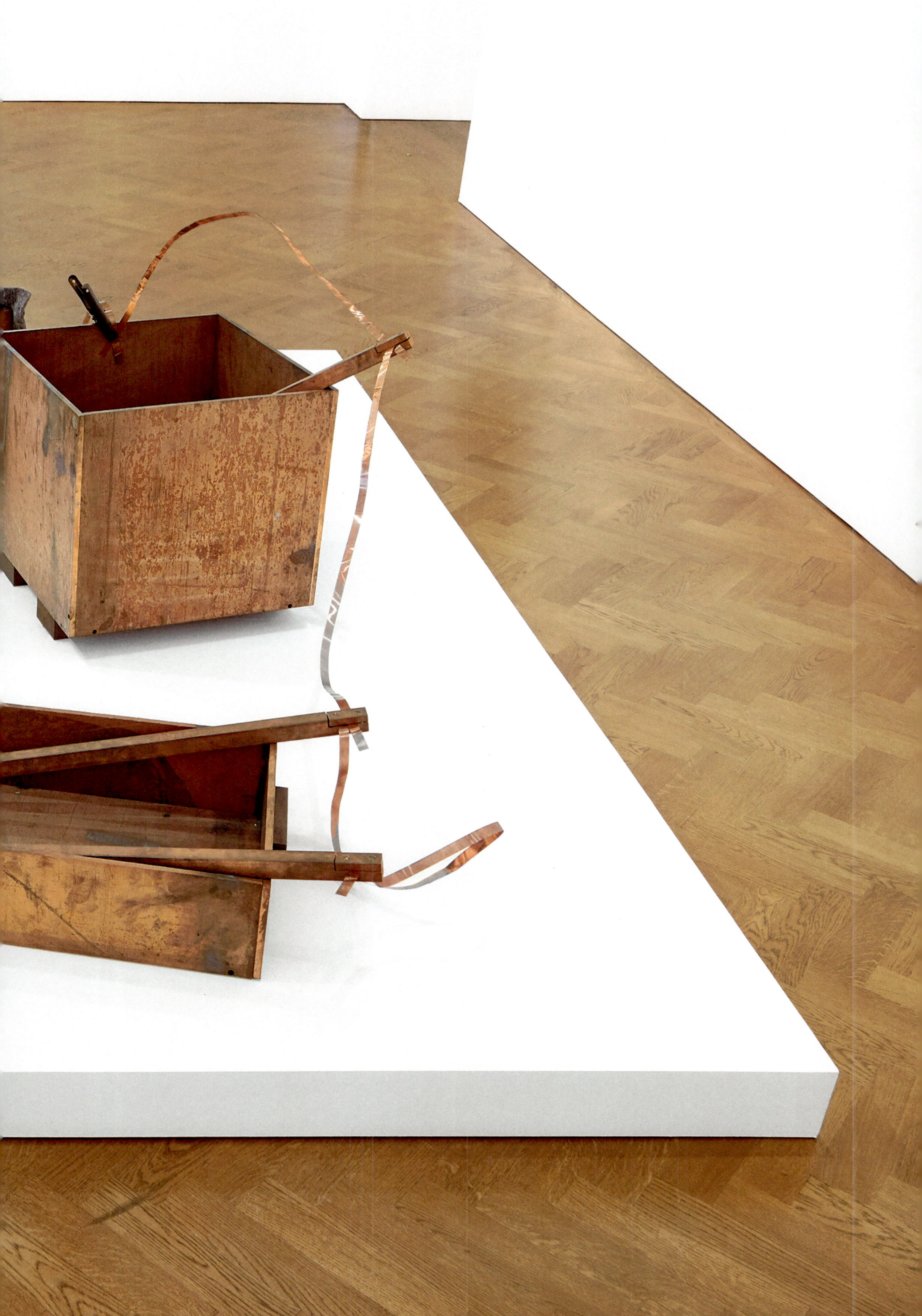

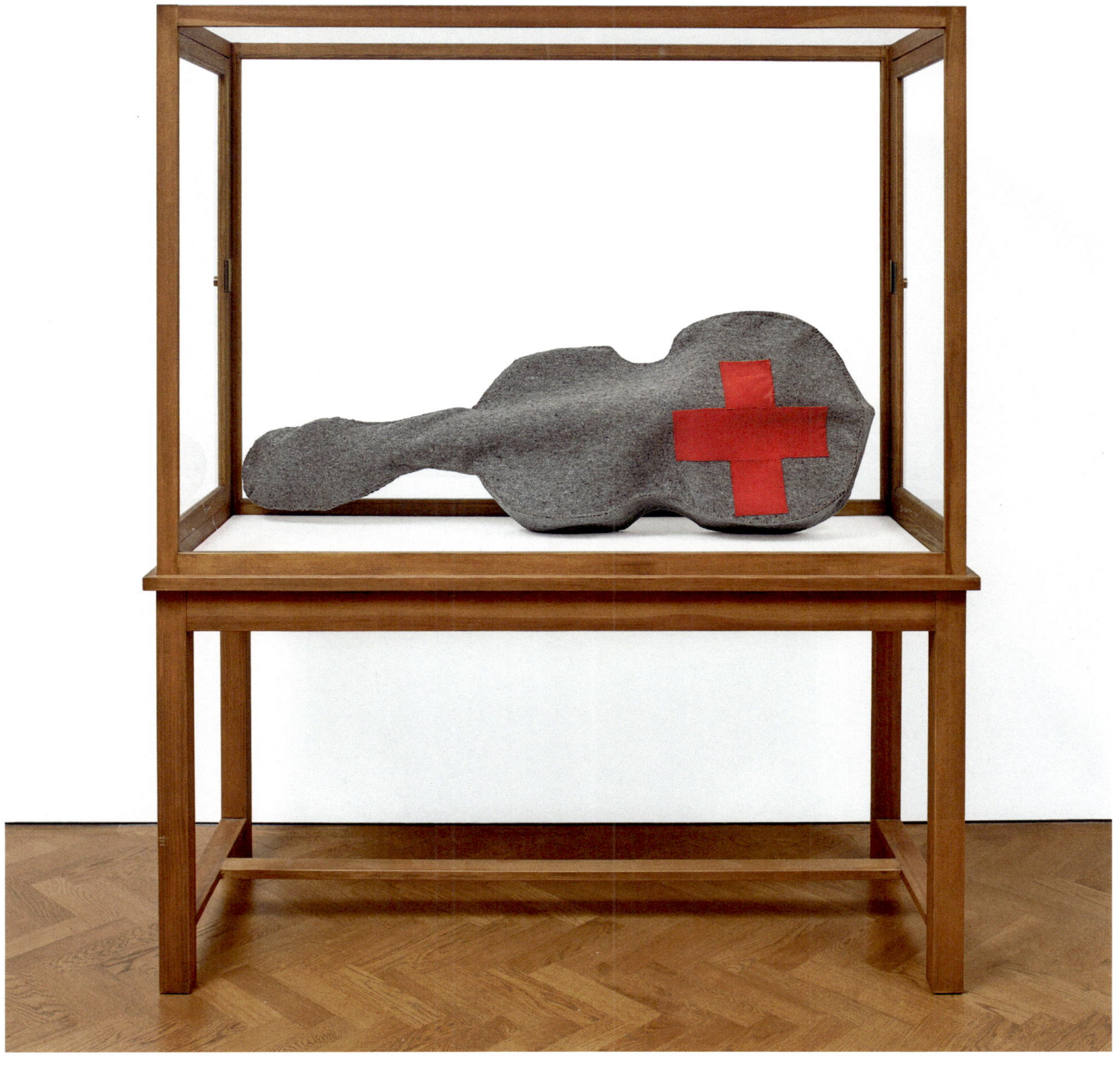

Infiltration-homogen für Cello
[Infiltration-homogeneous for Cello], 1966–85
Cello, felt and linen
47 x 142.5 x 27.5 cm (18.5 x 56.1 x 10.83 in)
Vitrine: 183 x 154.5 x 64 cm
(72.05 x 60.83 x 25.2 in)

Page 73
Filzanzug [Felt Suit], 1970
Felt
Approx. 170 x 60 cm (66.93 x 23.62 in)

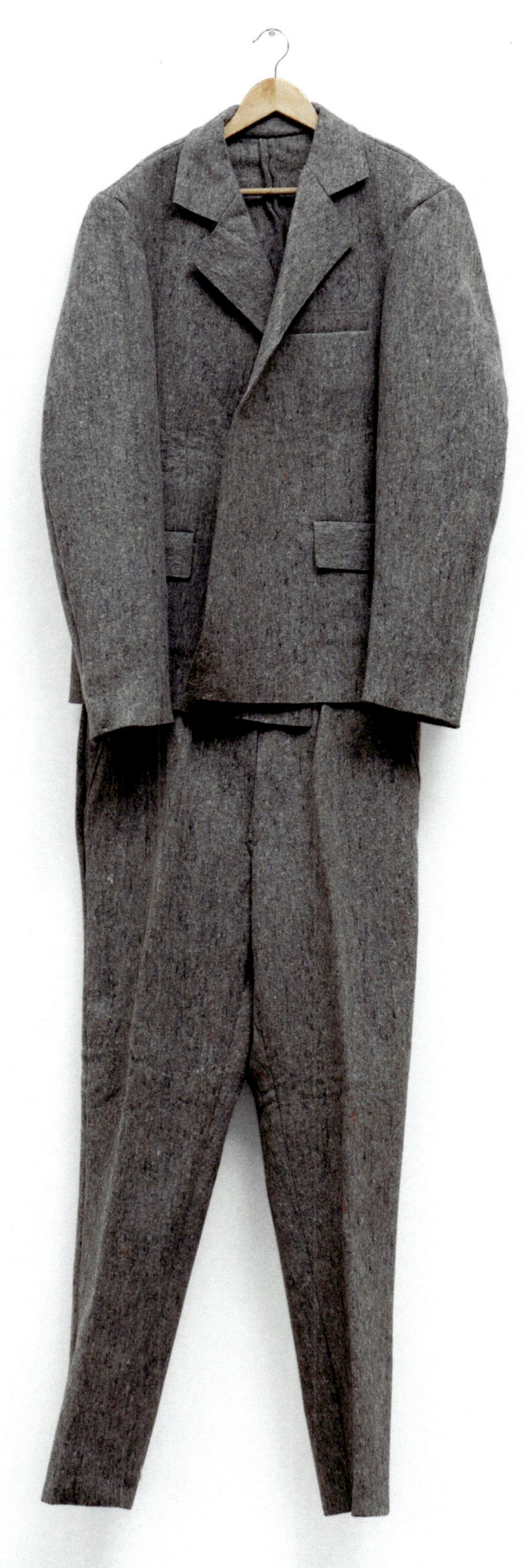

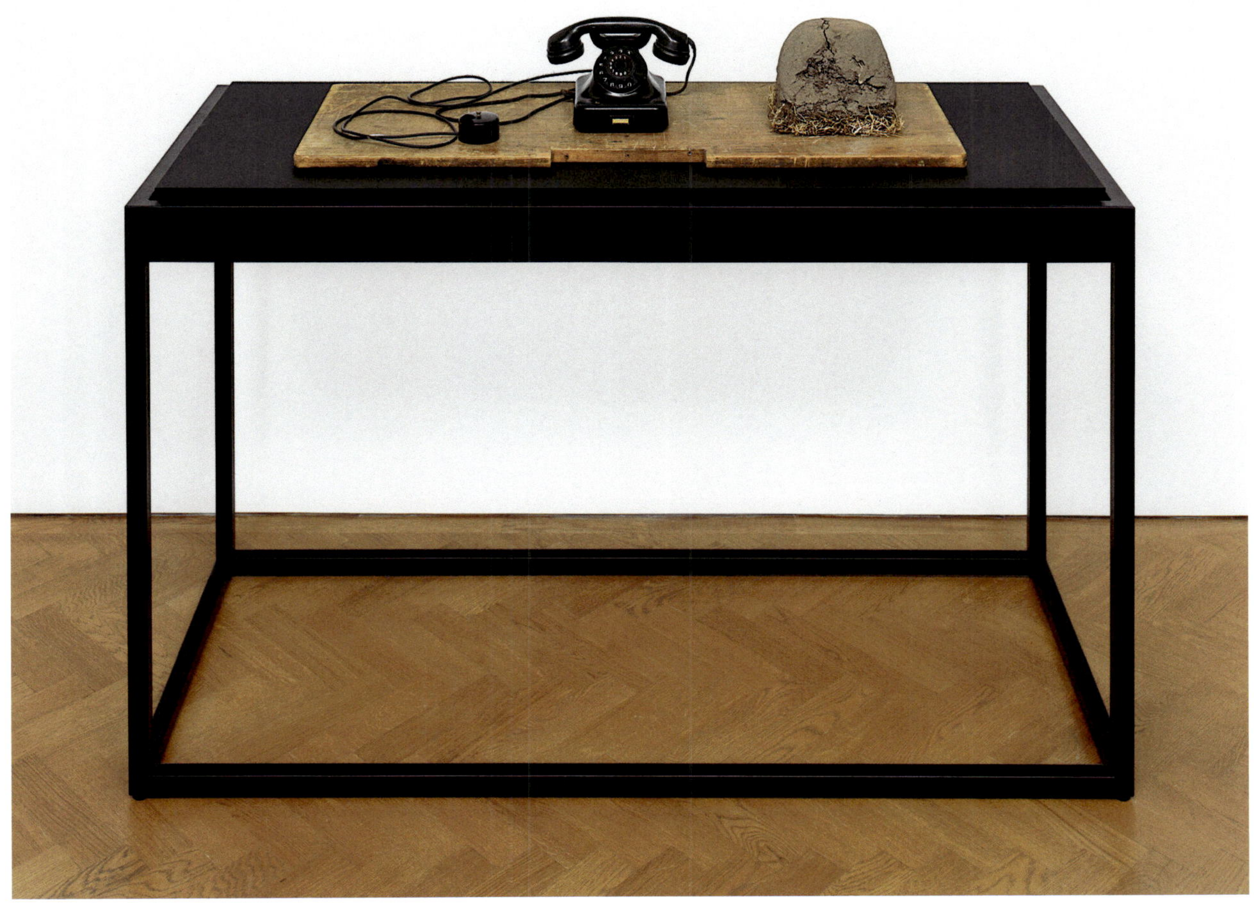

Erdtelefon [Earth Telephone], 1968
Telephone, clay lump, dried grass,
cable, wood board
19 x 104.5 x 38.5 cm (7.48 x 41.14 x 15.16 in)

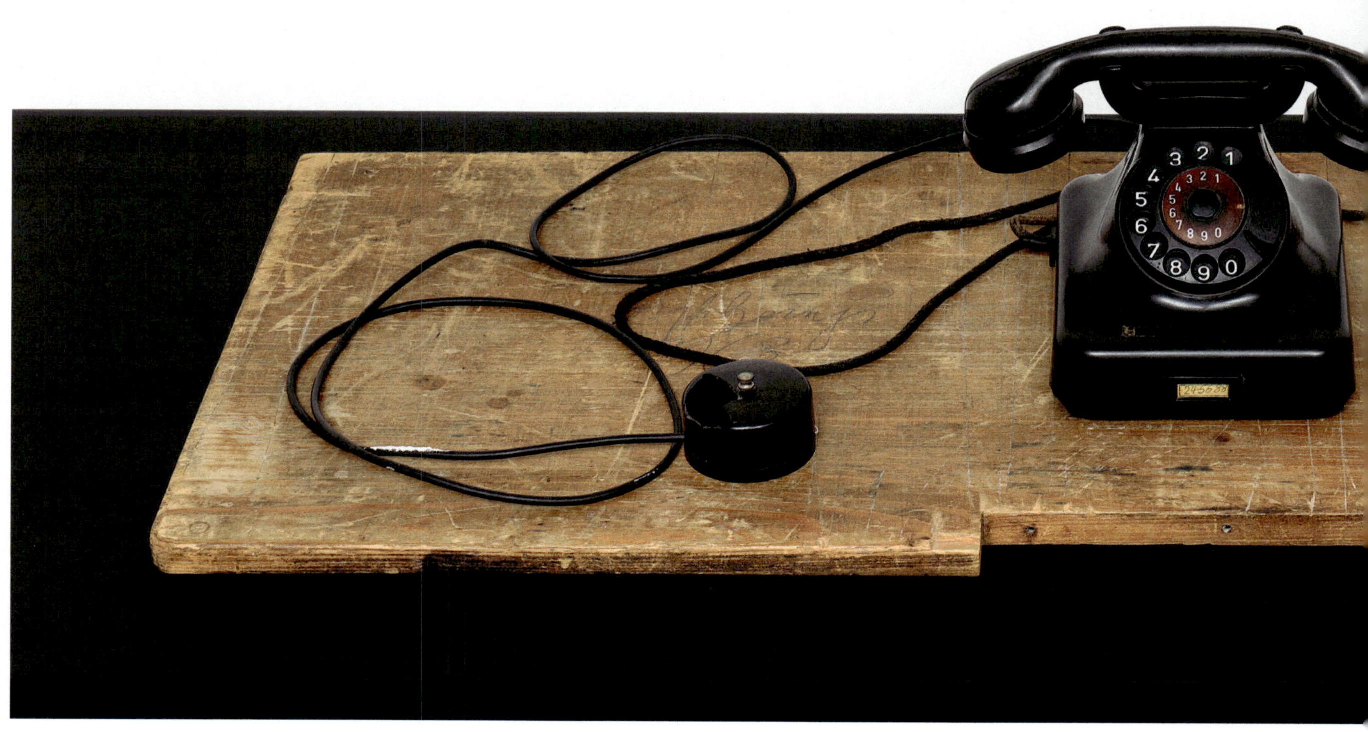

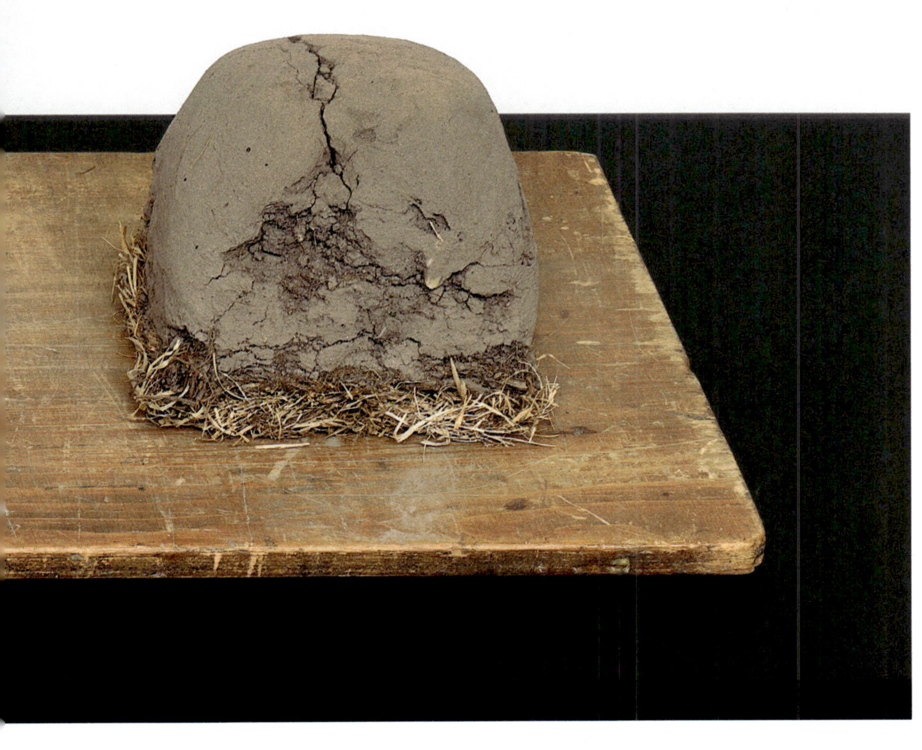

Erdtelefon [Earth Telephone], 1968

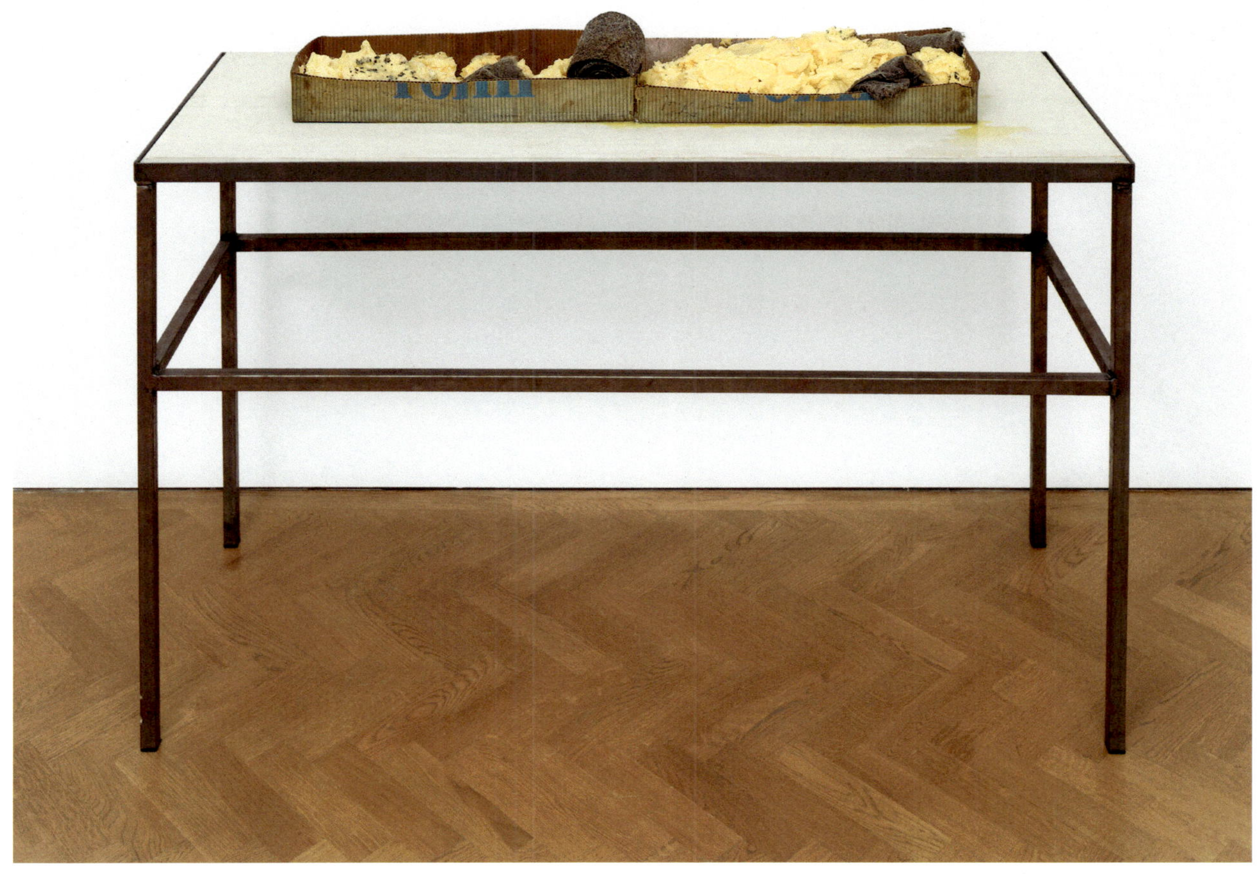

Aus dem Maschinenraum, Anhänger
[From the Machine Room, Trailer], 1977
'Romi' margarine and felt in cardboard boxes
16.5 x 111.8 x 31.8 cm (6.5 x 44.02 x 12.52 in)

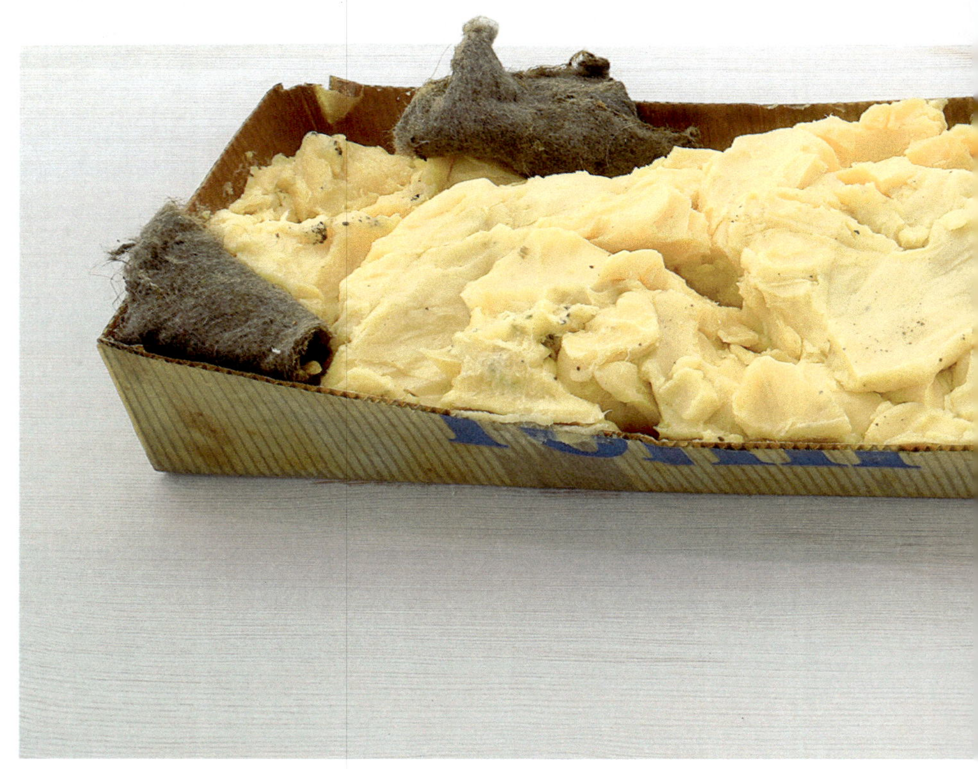

Aus dem Maschinenraum, Anhänger
[From the Machine Room, Trailer], 1977

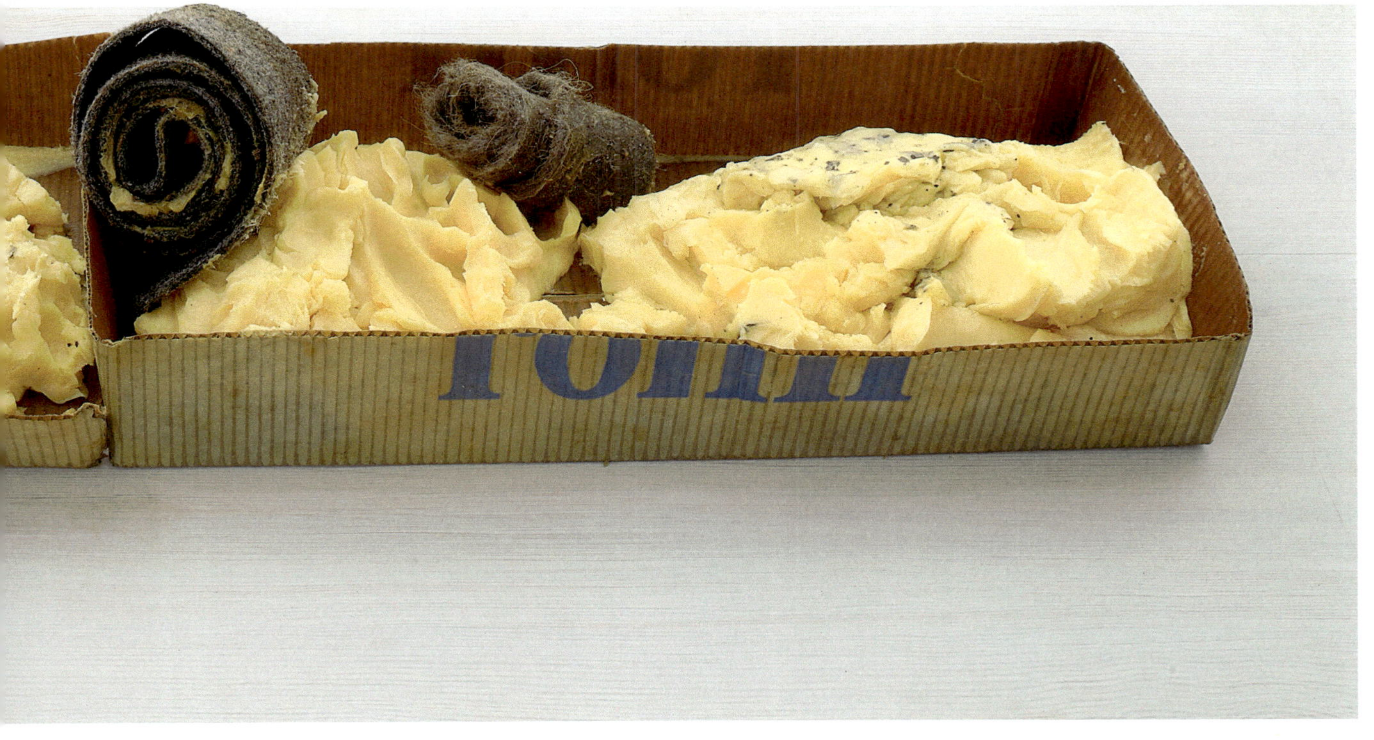

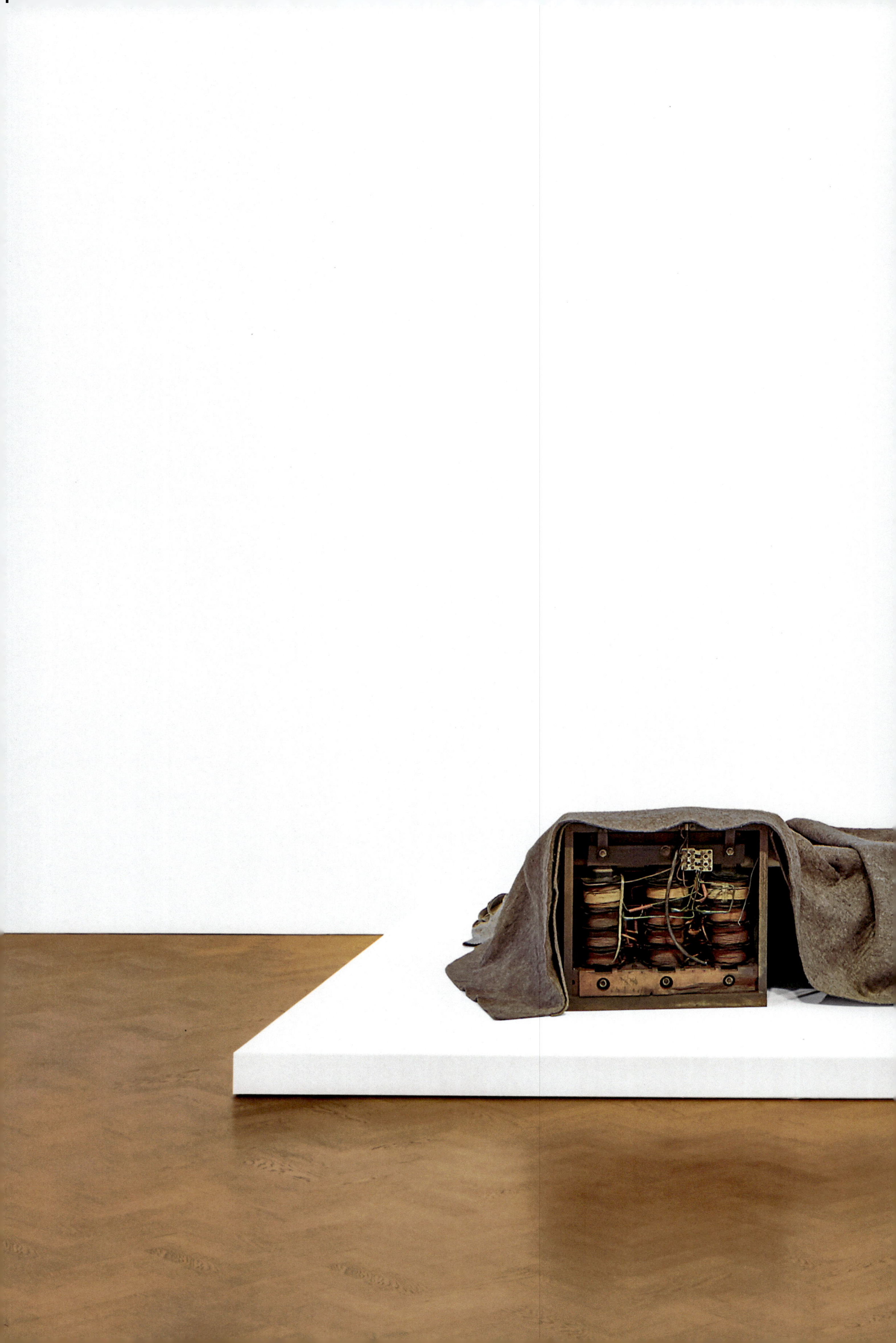

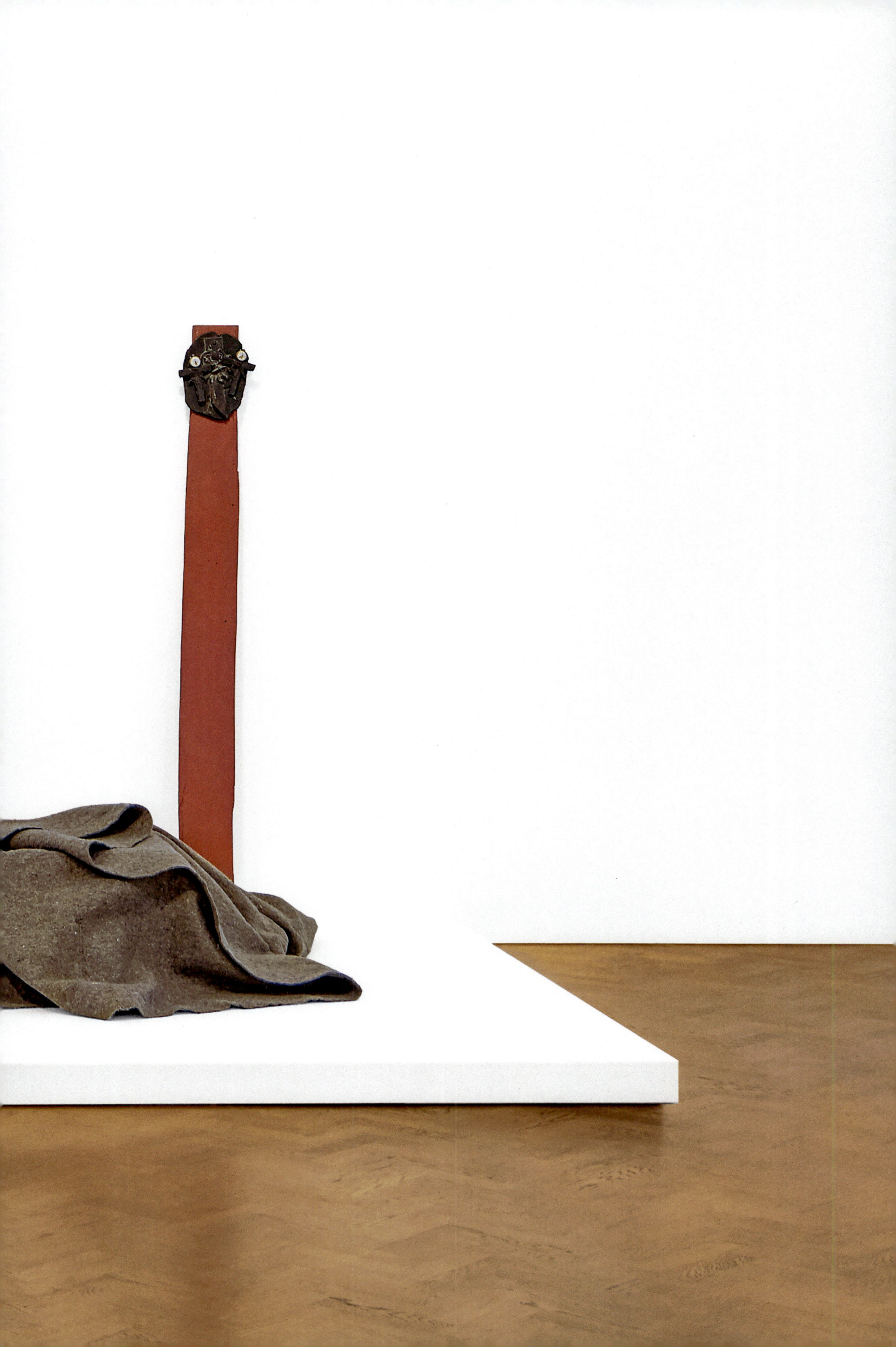

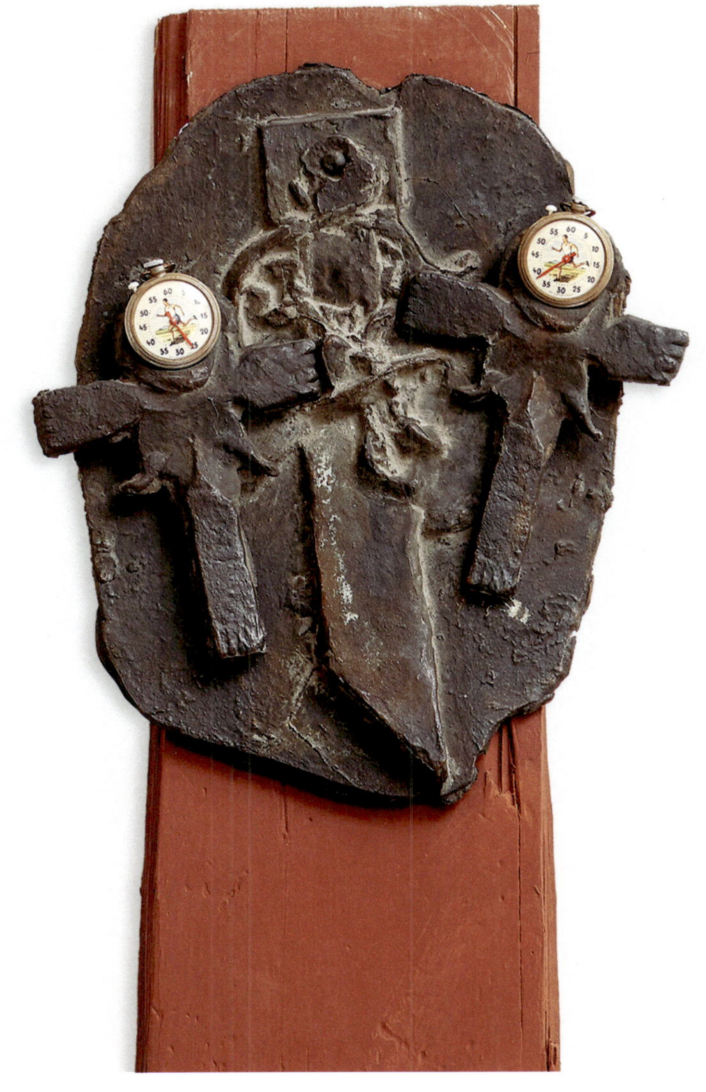

Pages 82–83
Feldbett [Campaign Bed], 1982
Electrical accumulator (copper, iron and wood) with campaign bed and felt blankets
61 x 241 x 193 cm (24.02 x 94.88 x 75.98 in)

3 Wurfkreuze mit 2 Spielstoppuhren
[3 Throwing Crosses with 2 Stopwatches], 1951–85
Bronze sculpture with stopwatches, wooden plank painted with oil (Braunkreuz)
Bronze sculpture: 33 x 29 cm (12.99 x 11.42 in)
Plank: 222 x 21 x 6 cm (87.4 x 8.27 x 2.36 in)

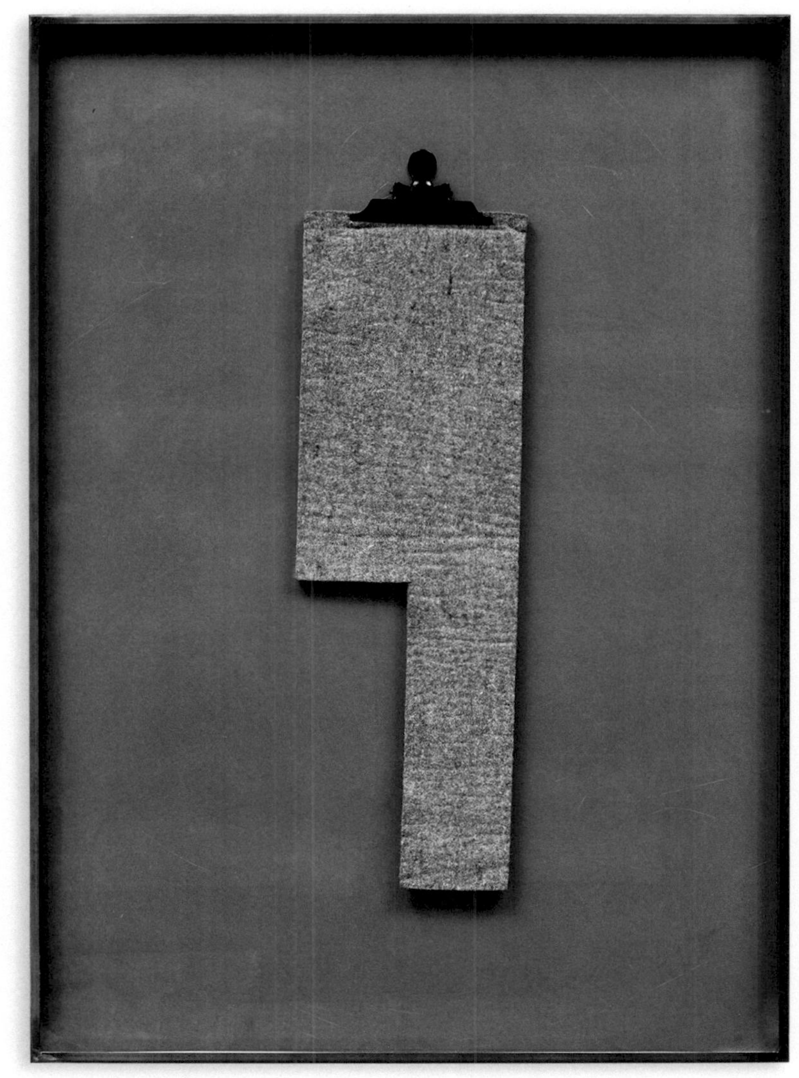

Evolutionäre Schwelle
[Threshold of Evolution], 1985
Felt and metal clamp
Framed: 110.5 x 80.4 x 4.5 cm
(43.5 x 31.65 x 1.77 in)

Pages 88–89
Evolutionäre Schwelle
[Threshold of Evolution], 1985
8 felt pieces, each uniquely cut, black clamps
Installed: 200 x 442 cm (78.74 x 174.02 in)

Page 89
Hasenstein [Hare Stone], 1982
Basalt stone, gold spray-paint
40 x 160 x 45 cm (15.75 x 63 x 17.72 in)

Schlitten [Sled], 1969
Wooden sled, felt, cloth straps, torch, wax and cord
35 x 90 x 35 cm (13.78 x 35.43 x 13.78 in)

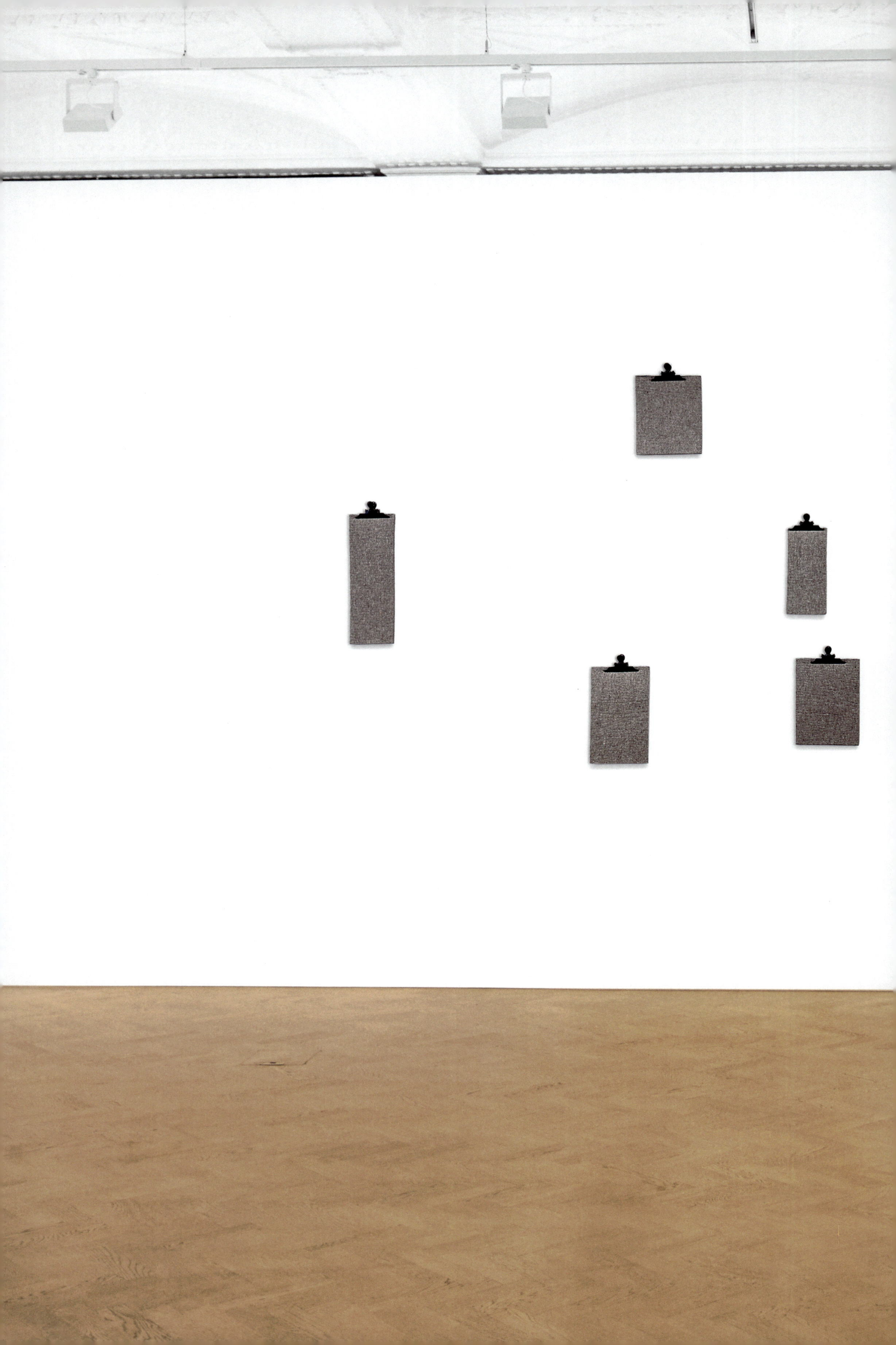

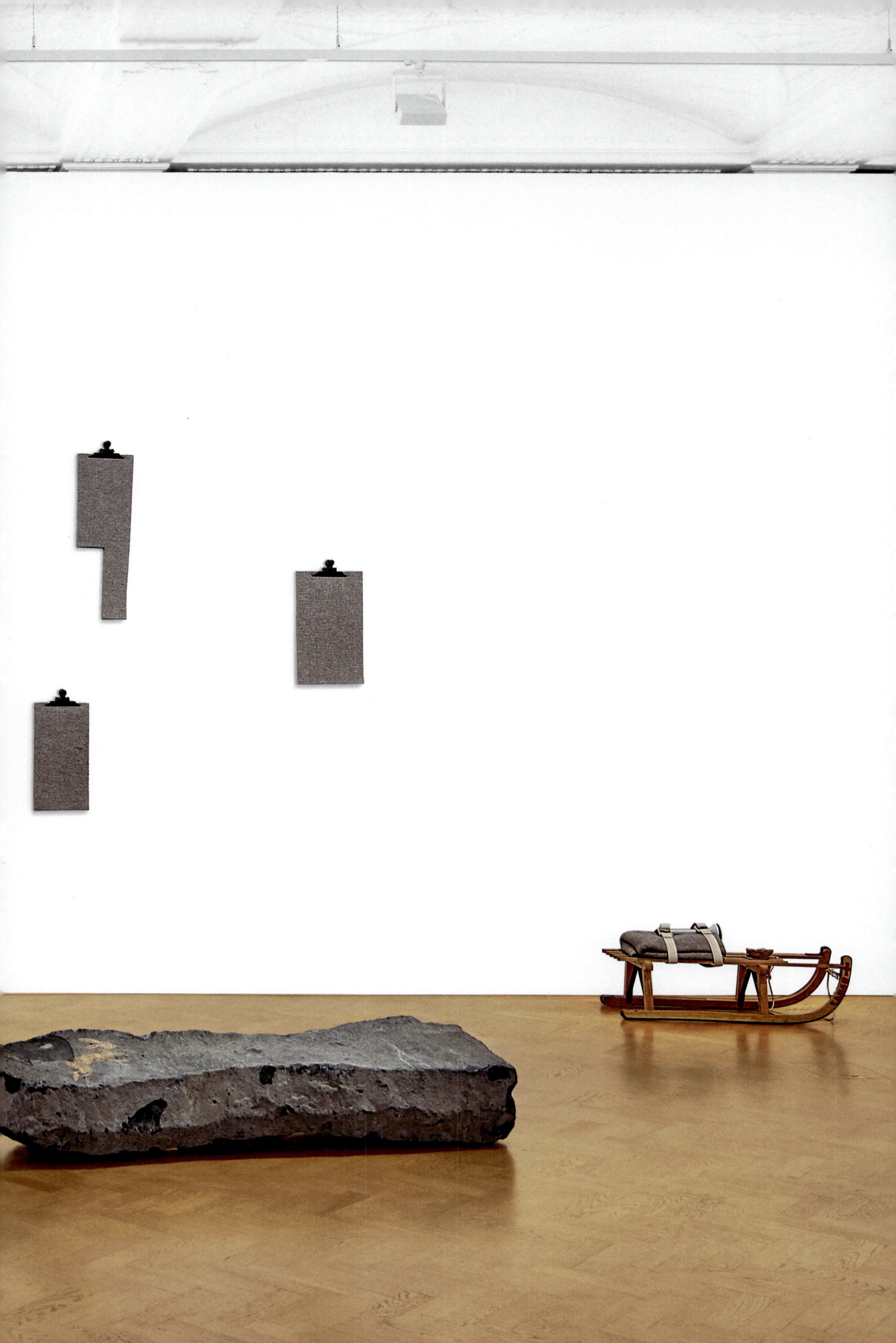

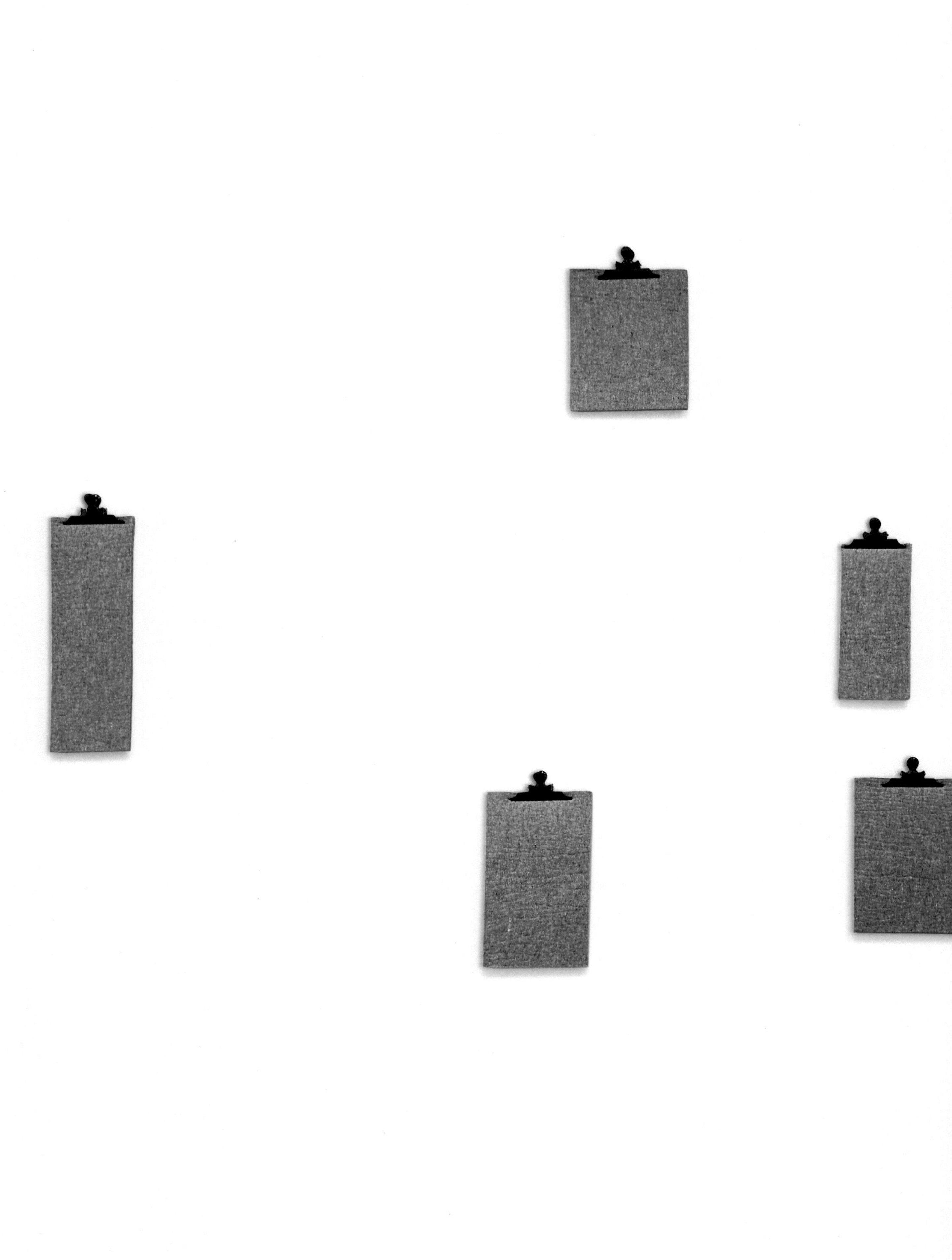

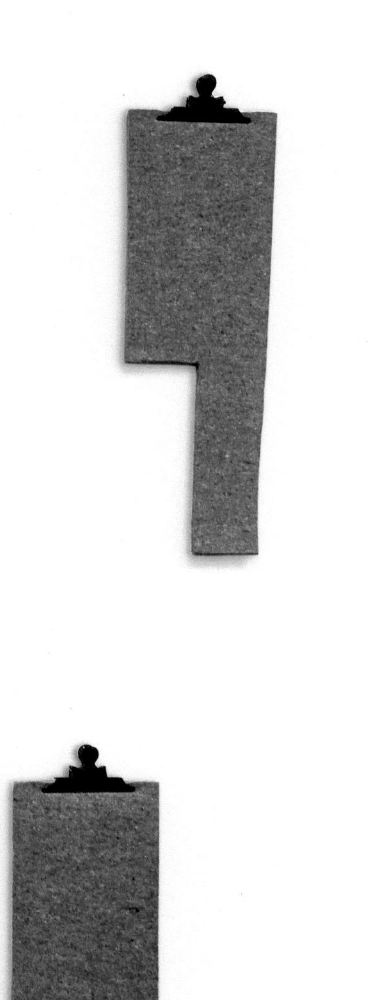

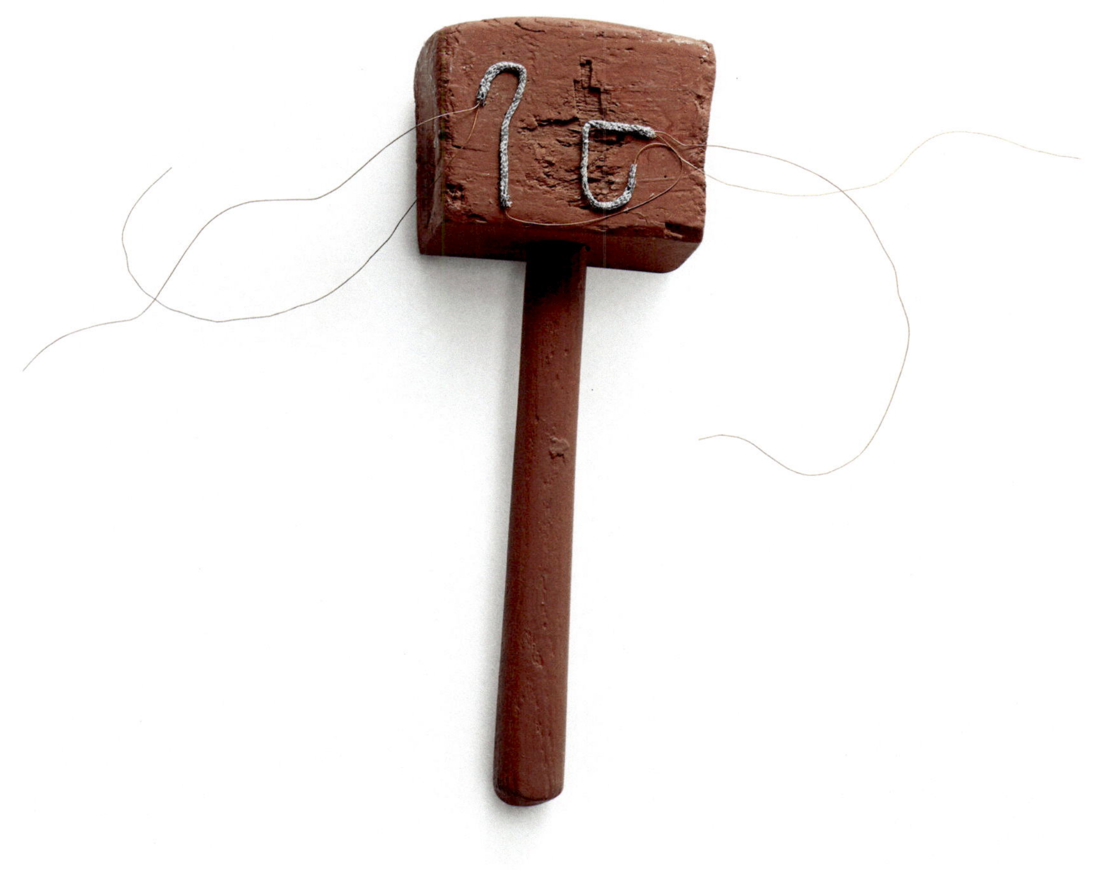

Pages 90–91
Evolutionäre Schwelle
[Threshold of Evolution], 1985

Thor's Hammer, 1961–62
Wooden mallet painted with oil
(Braunkreuz) with wire attachments
43 x 16 x 7 cm (16.93 x 6.3 x 2.76 in)

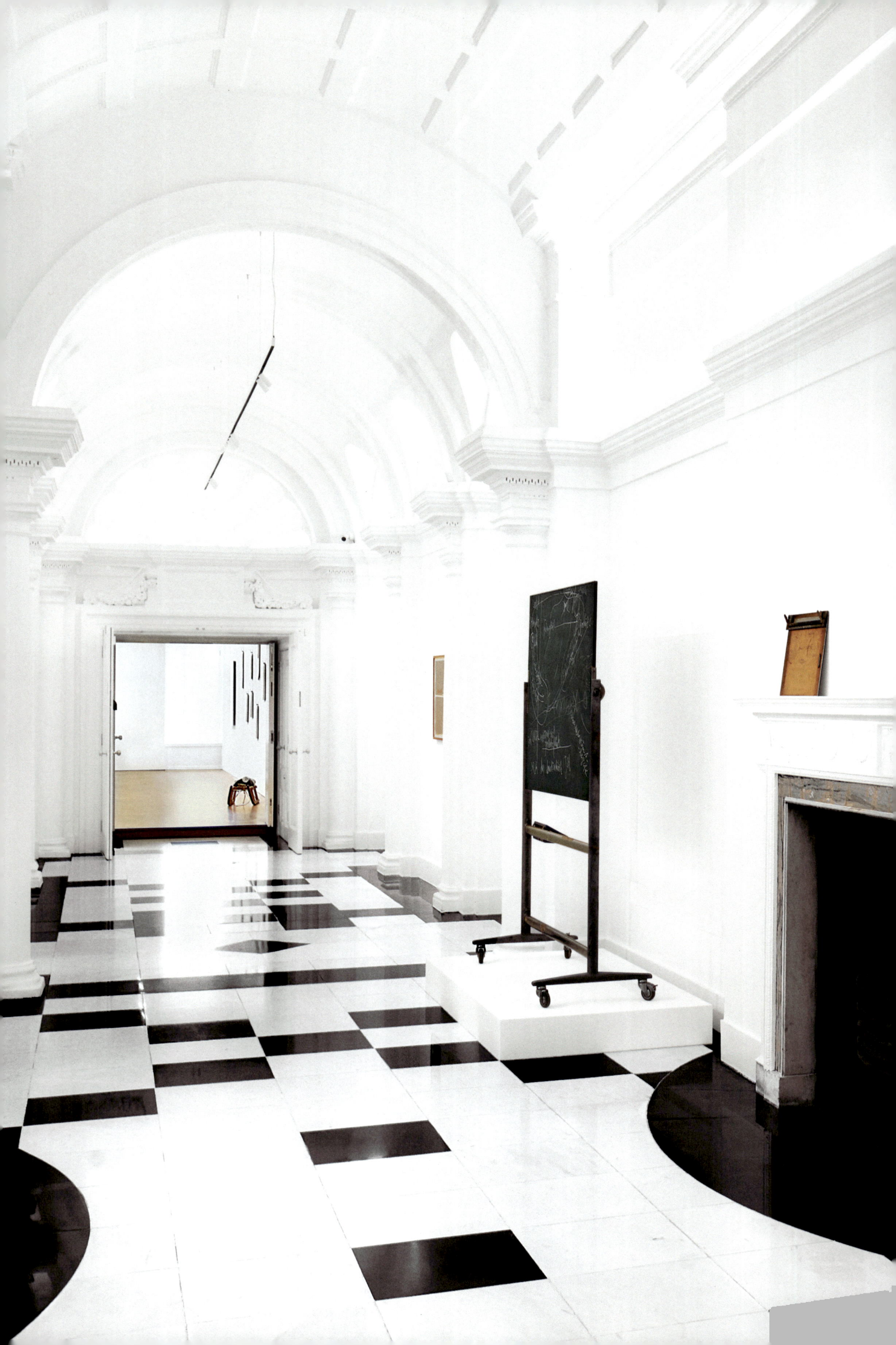

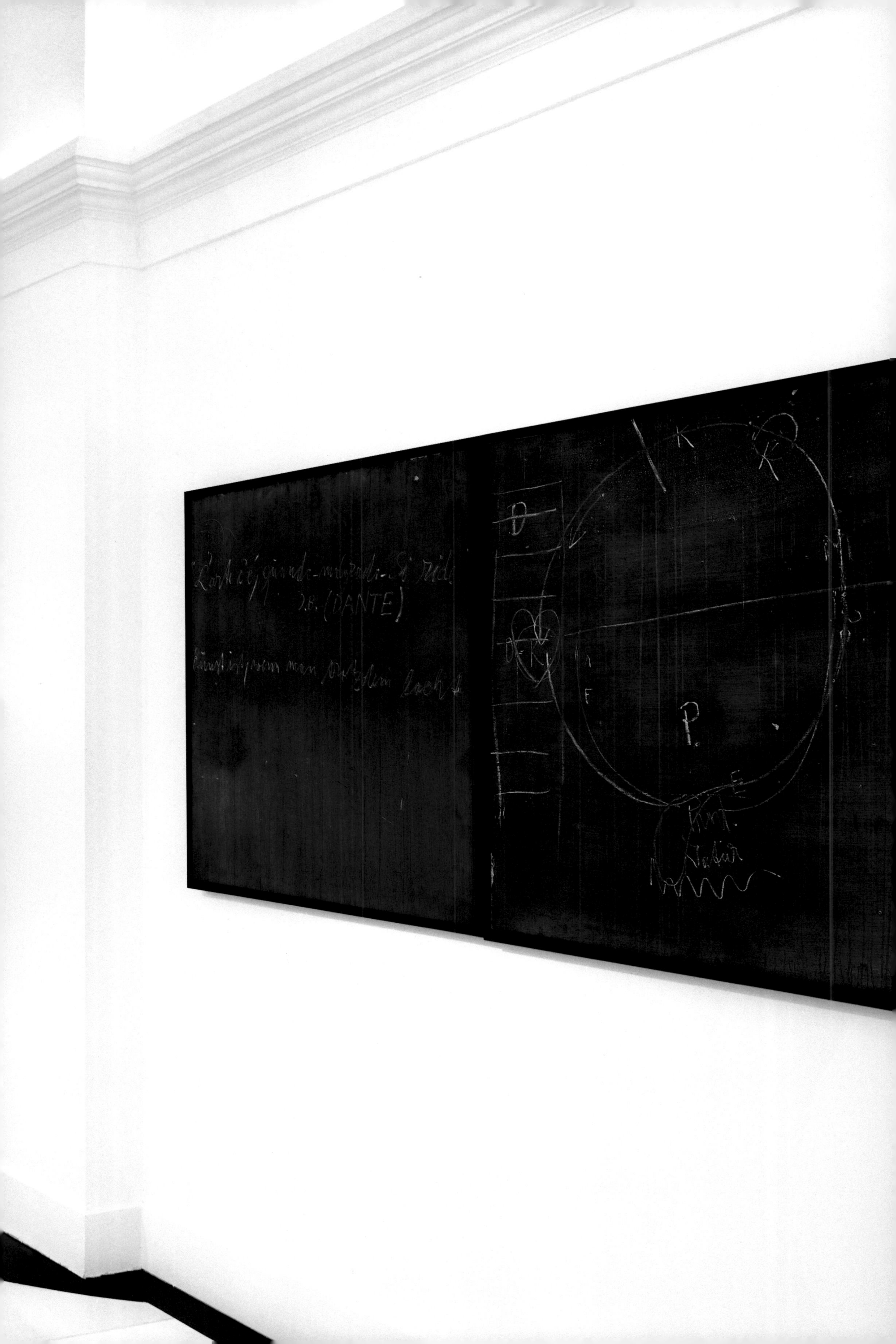
(DANTE)
P.

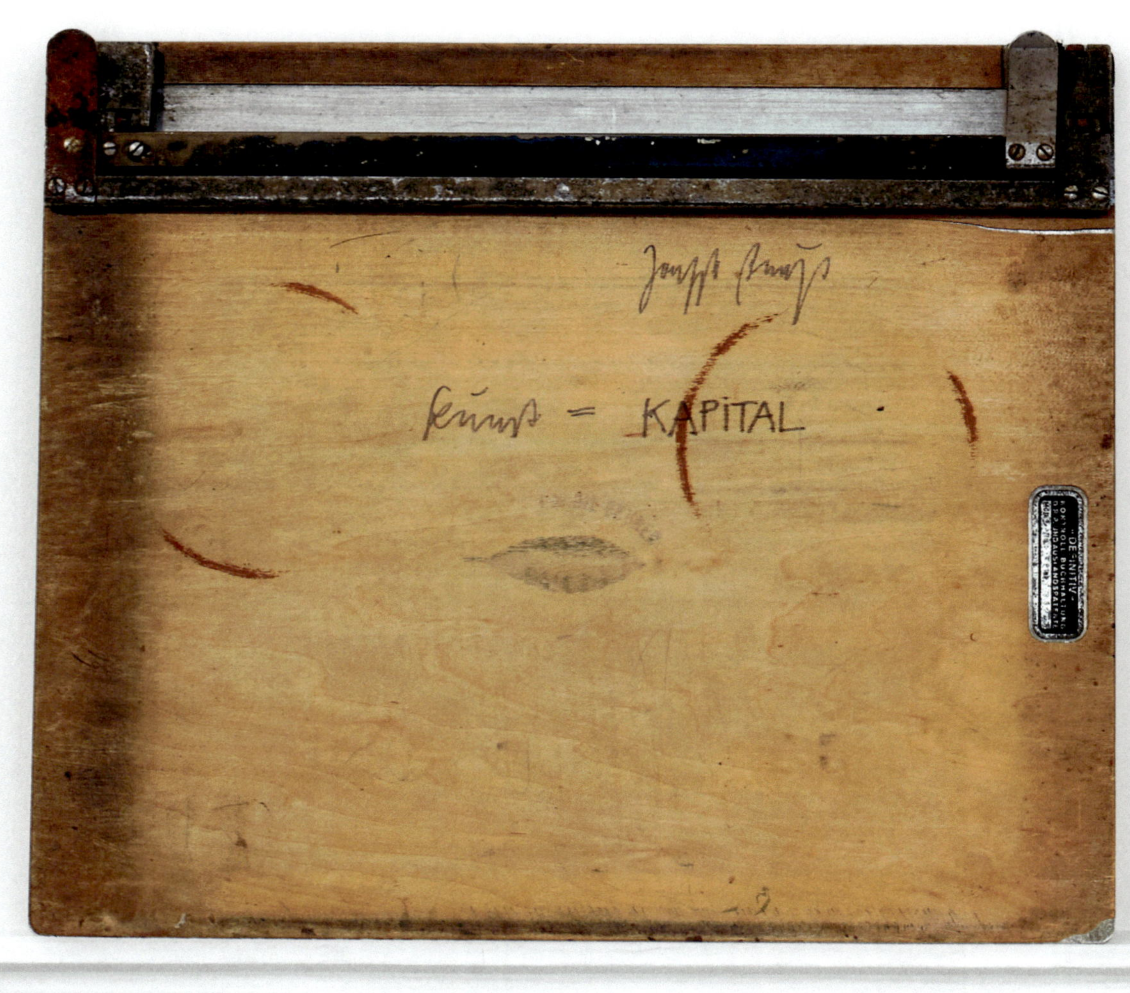
Kunst = KAPITAL

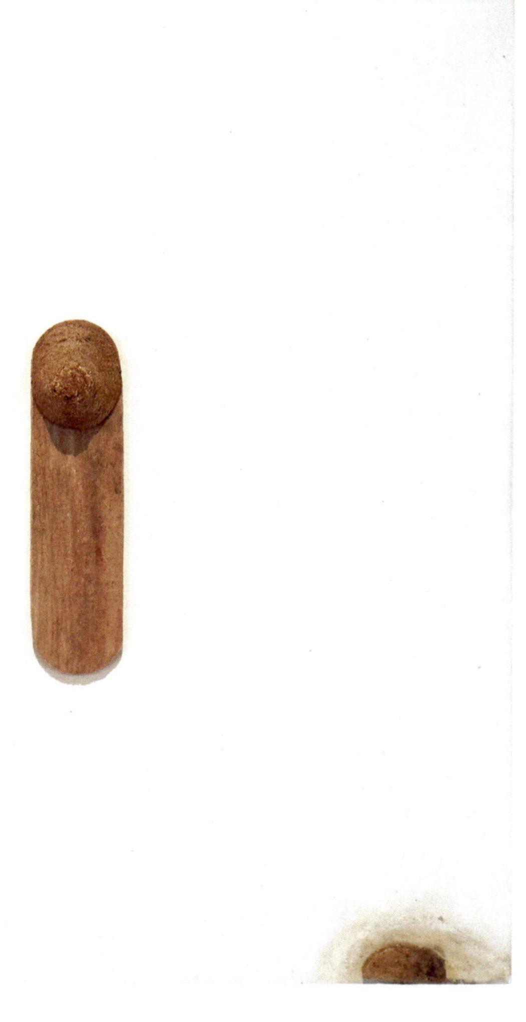

Page 96
KUNST=KAPITAL [ART = CAPITAL], ca. 1983
Felt-tip pen and stamp 'FÜR DIE GRÜNEN' [FOR THE GREENS] on clipboard
32 x 38 x 3.8 cm (12.6 x 14.96 x 1.5 in)

Brustwarze, 1963
Plaster panel, small wooden board, crushed and glued plant matter
50 x 45 x 5 cm (19.68 x 17.7 x 1.9 in)

Pages 100–101
Ökologie und Sozialismus
[Ecology and Socialism], 1980
Chalk, double-sided blackboard, tray and metal stand (back and front)
Overall: 189.9 x 138.4 x 61 cm
(74.76 x 54.49 x 24.02 in)
Blackboard: 99.7 x 128.9 cm (39.25 x 50.75 in)

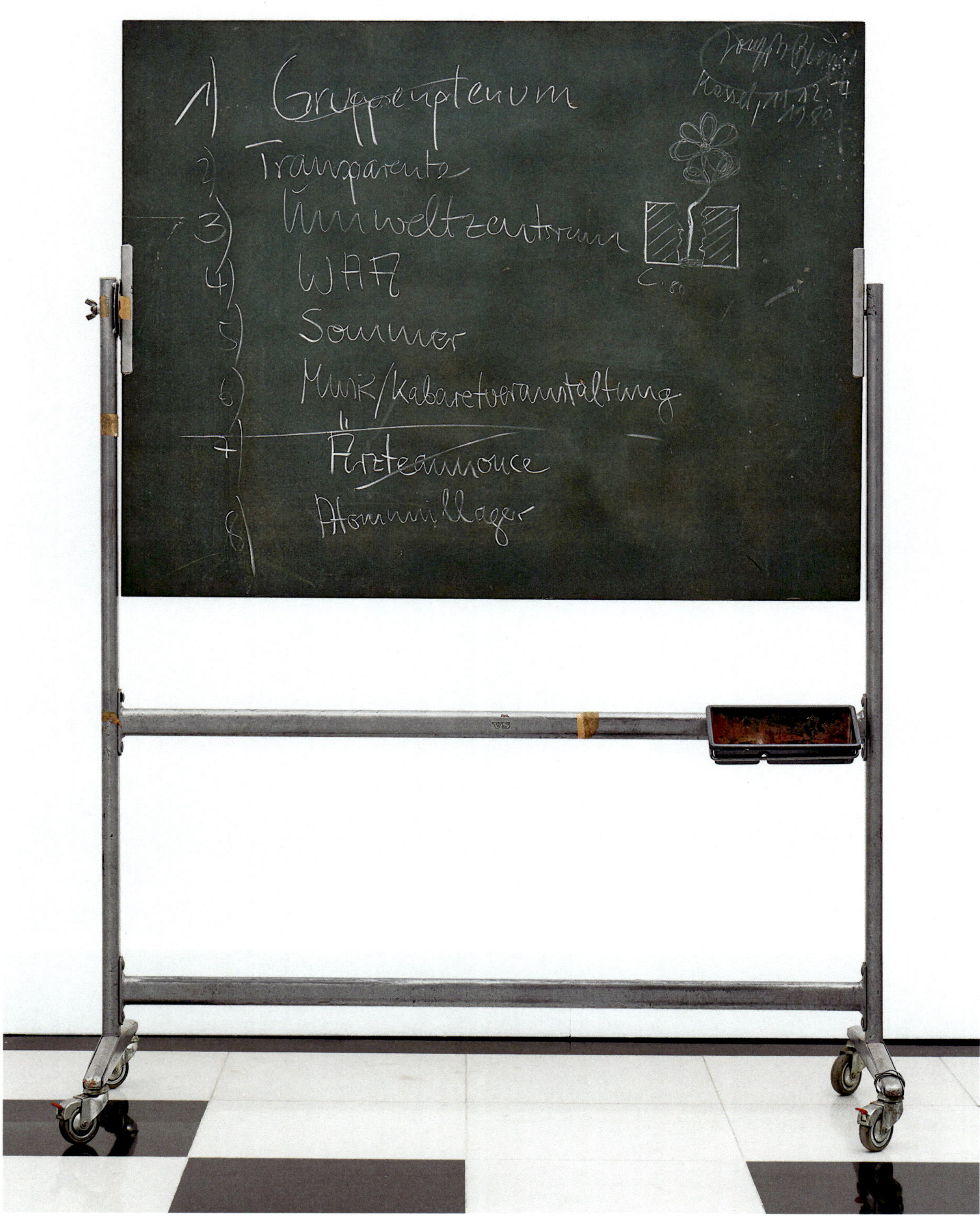
1) Gruppenplenum
2) Transparente
3) Umweltzentrum
4) WAA
5) Sommer
6) Musik/Kabaretveranstaltung
8) Atommüllager

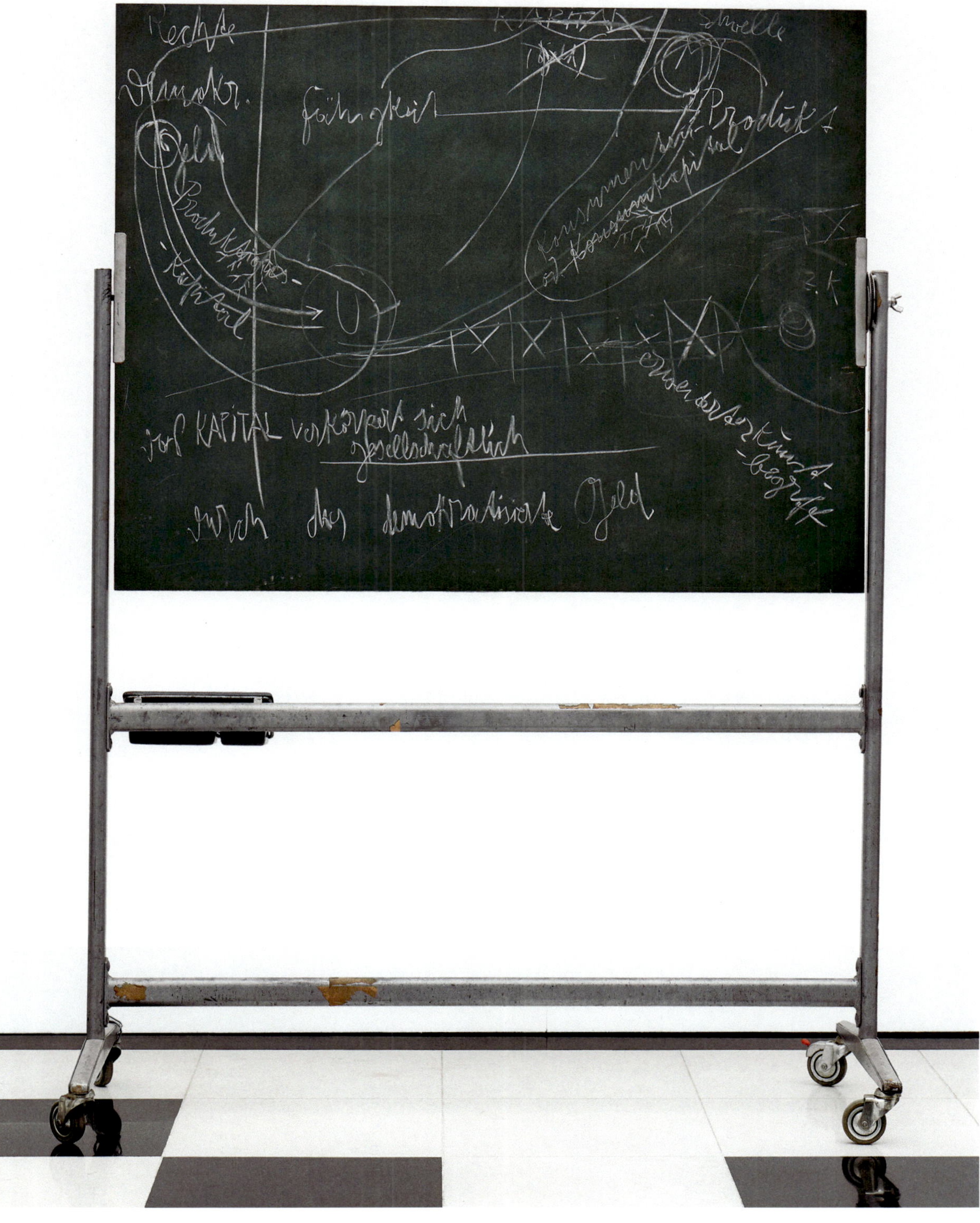
Schwelle
Fähigkeit
Produkt
Geld
KAPITAL
gesellschaftlich
Geld

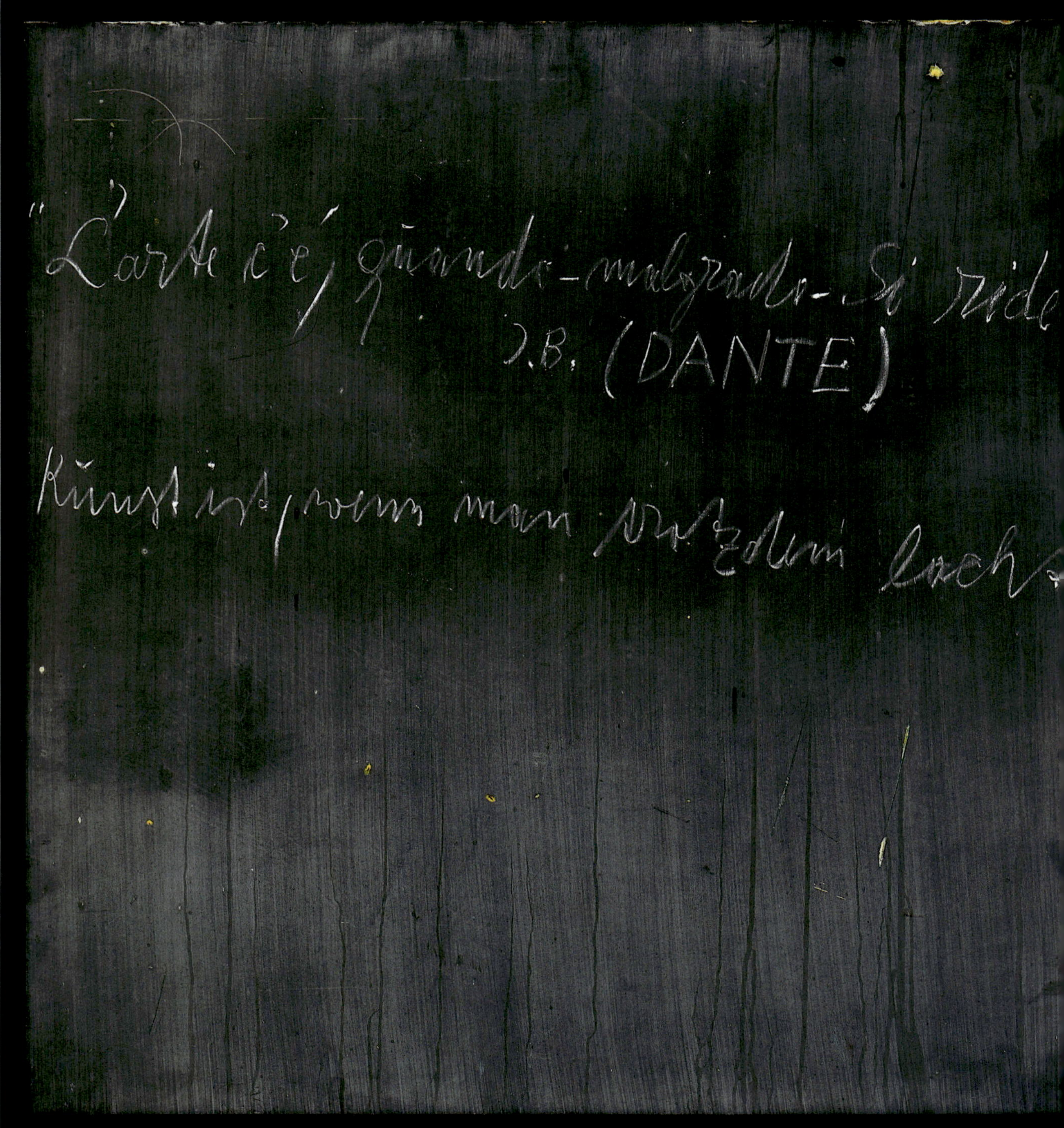
"L'arte c'è quando – malgrado – si ride
J.B. (DANTE)
Kunst ist, wenn man trotzdem lach

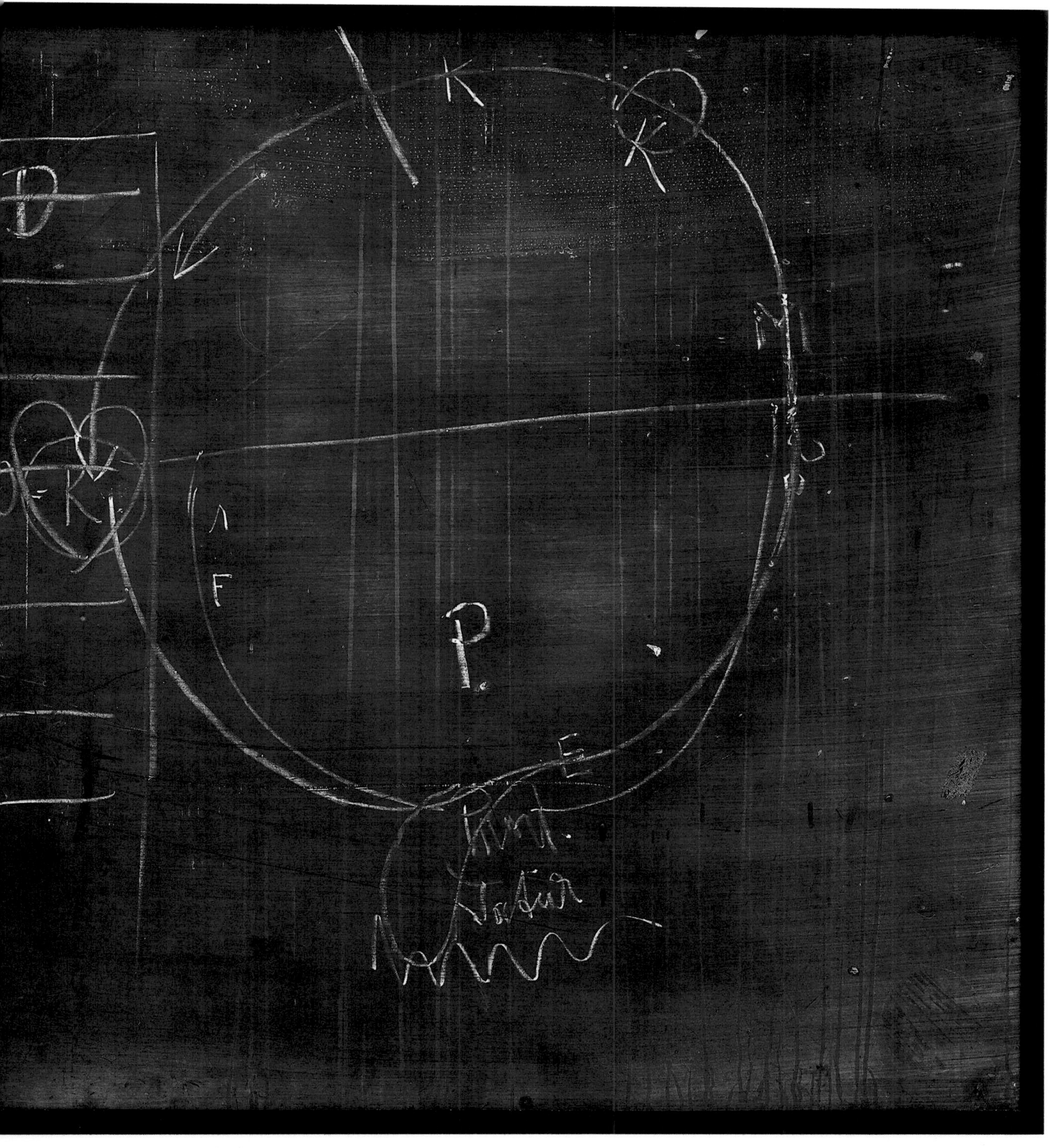

Kunst ist, wenn man trotzdem lacht
[Art is when you laugh despite everything], 1979
Chalk on blackboard, in two parts
Each blackboard: 102 x 103 cm (40.16 x 40.55 in)

Page 105
La rivoluzione siamo Noi
[We Are the Revolution], 1972
Silkscreen with handwritten text and stamp
183 x 91 cm (75.2 x 39.37 in)

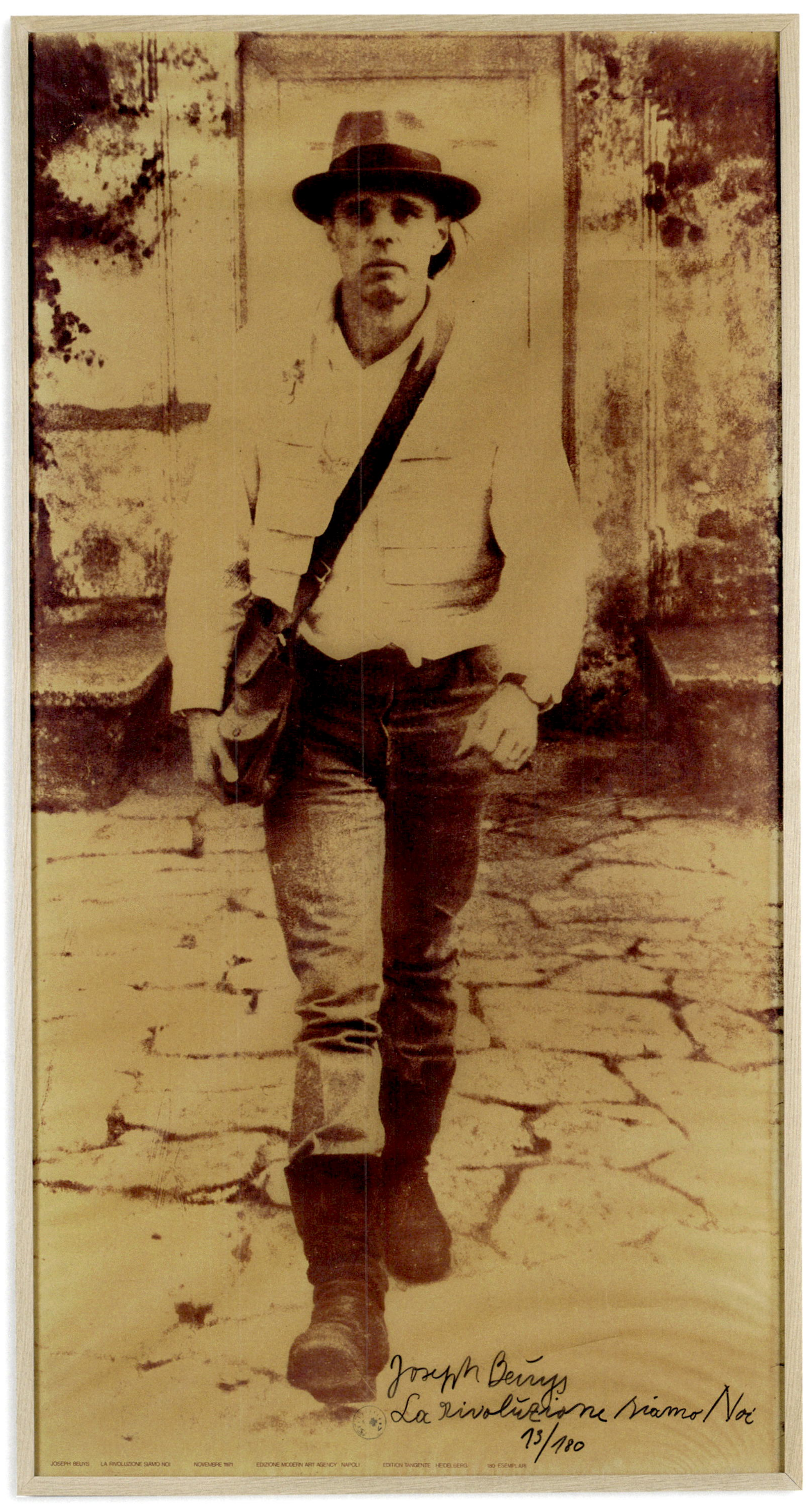
Joseph Beuys
La rivoluzione siamo Noi
13/180
JOSEPH BEUYS LA RIVOLUZIONE SIAMO NOI NOVEMBRE 1971 EDIZIONE MODERN ART AGENCY NAPOLI EDITION TANGENTE HEIDELBERG 180 ESEMPLARI

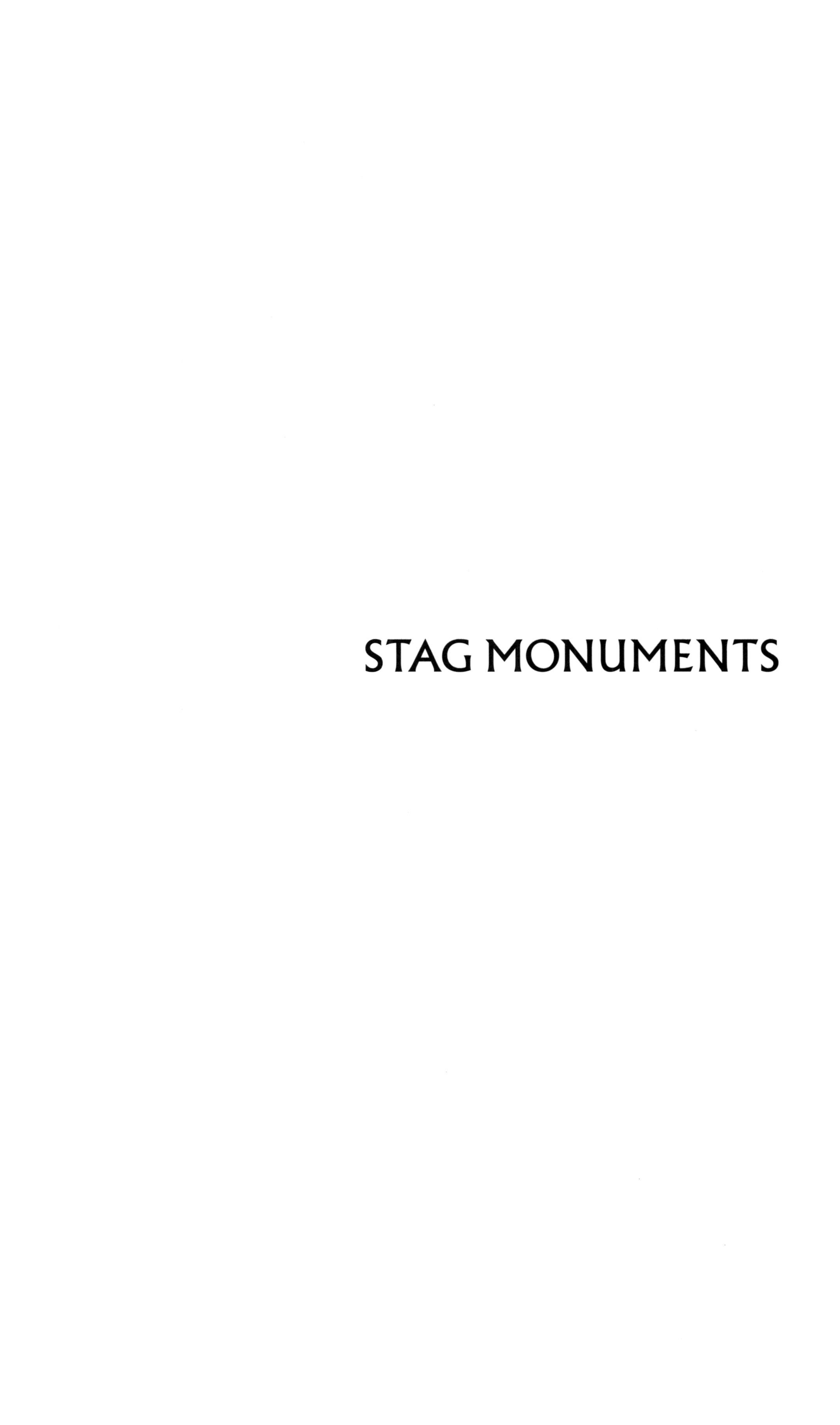

STAG MONUMENTS

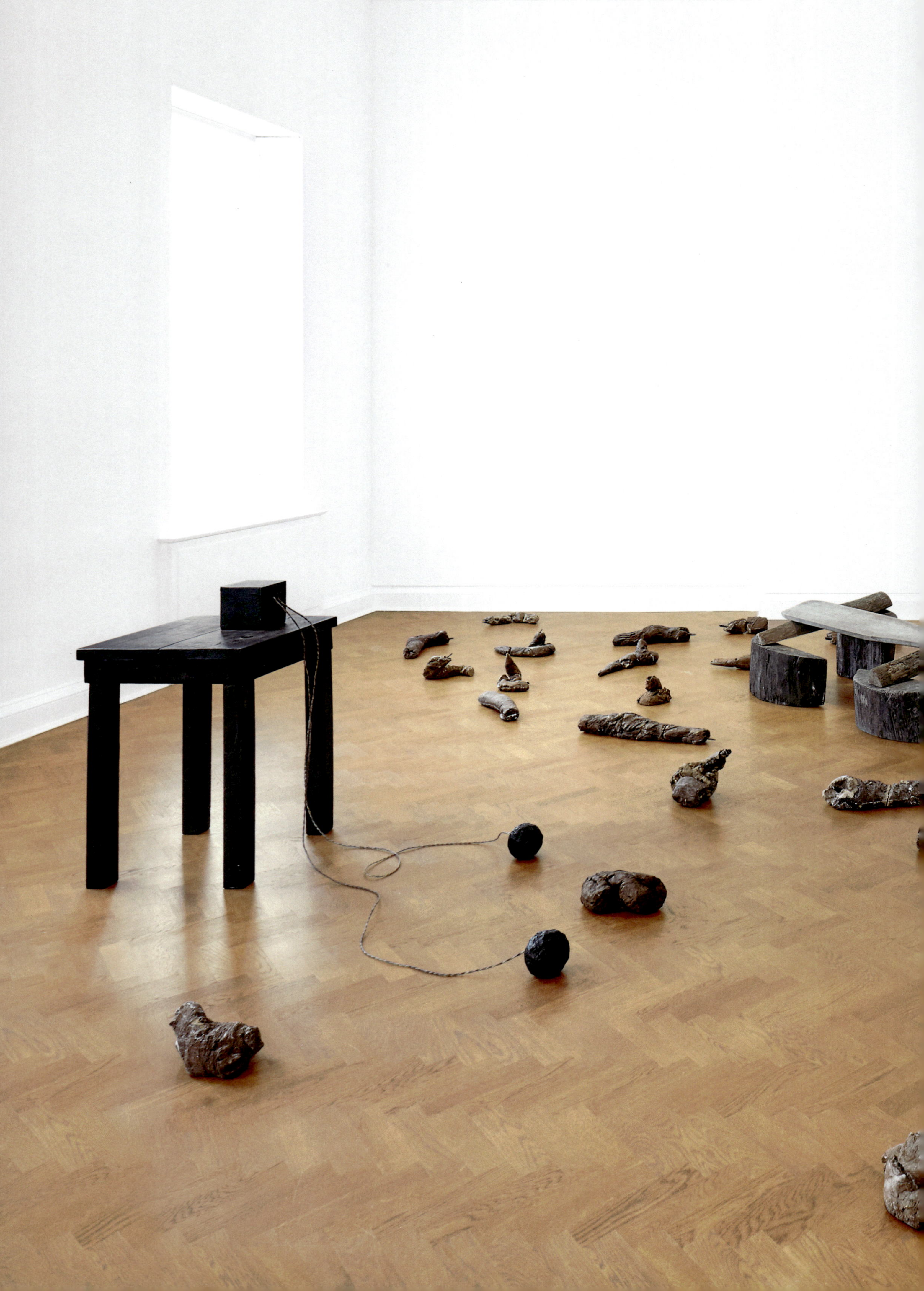

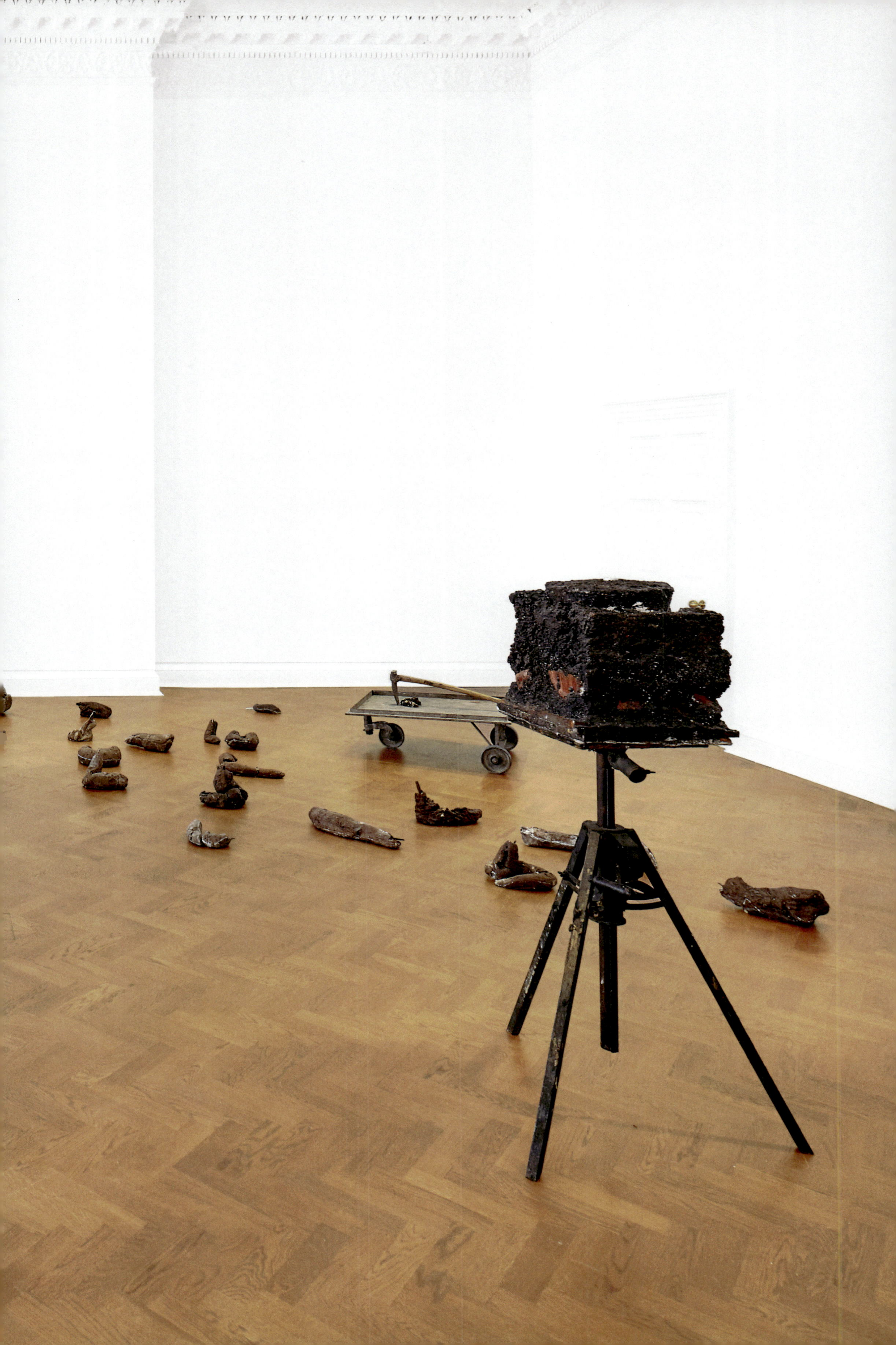

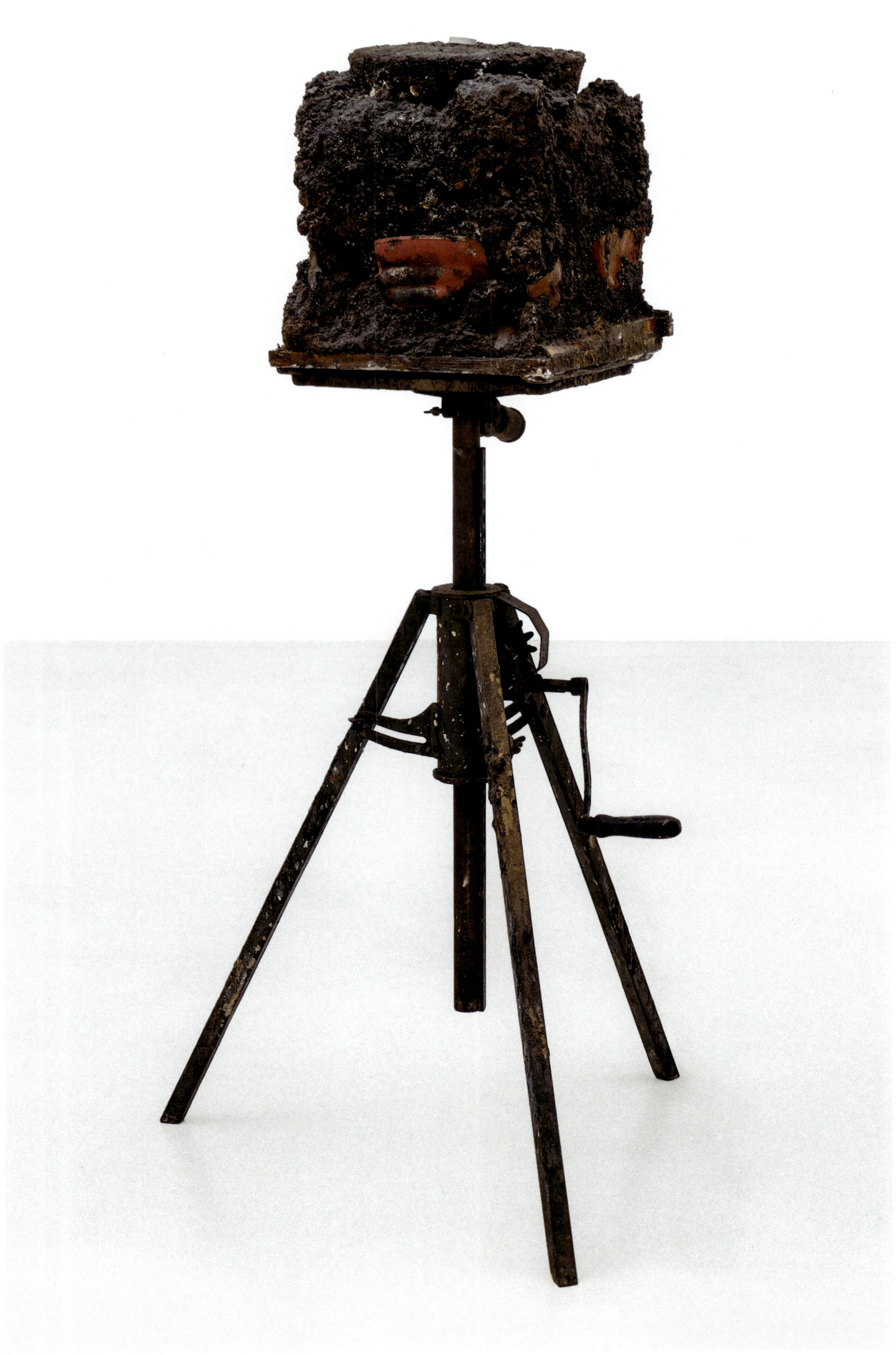

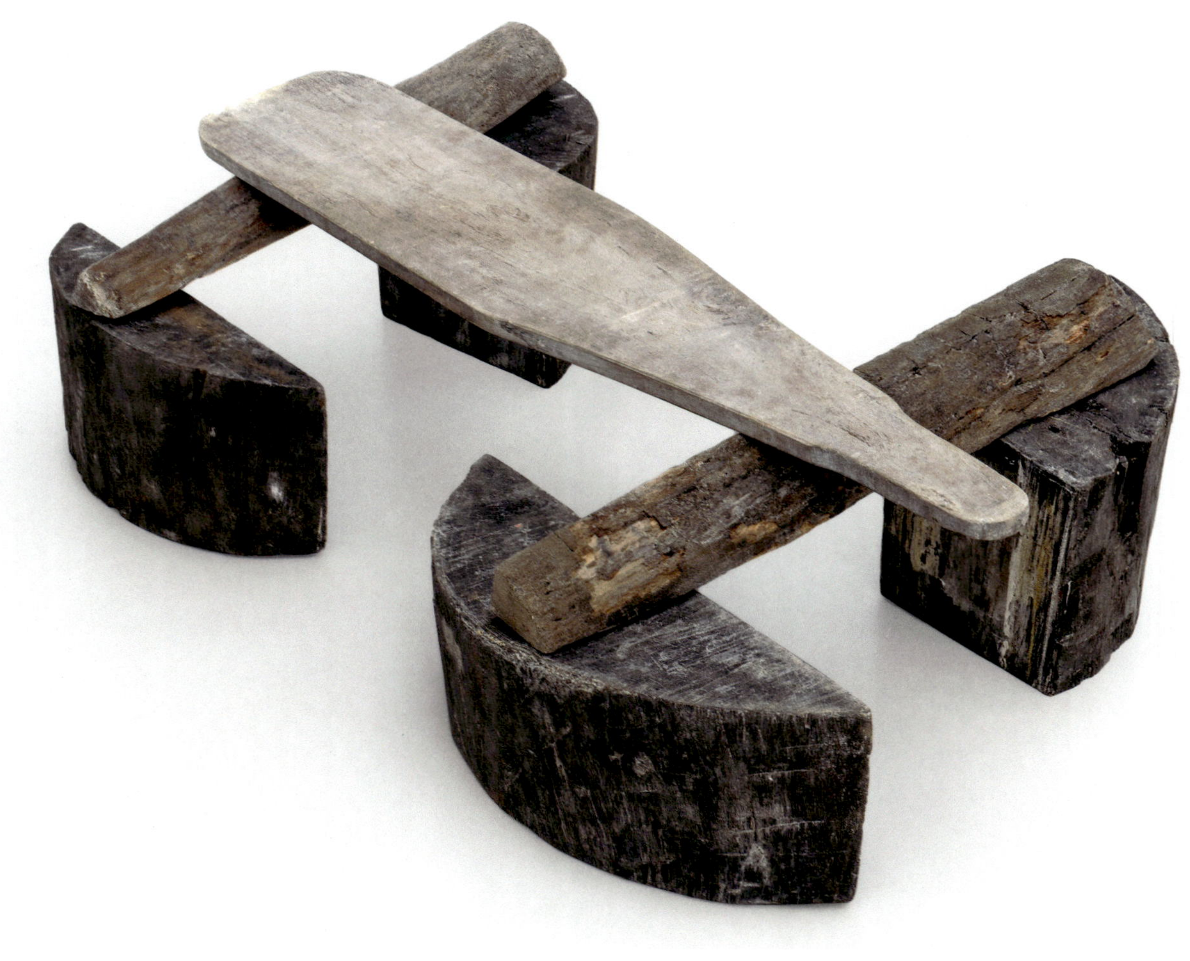

Page 111
Boothia Felix, 1958/1982
Metal tripod, terracotta shards, earth, rosemary roots, compass
143 x 75 x 75 cm (56.3 x 29.53 x 29.53 in)

Hirsch [Stag], 1958/1982
Teak wood and wooden ironing board
48 x 172 x 104 cm (18.9 x 67.72 x 40.94 in)

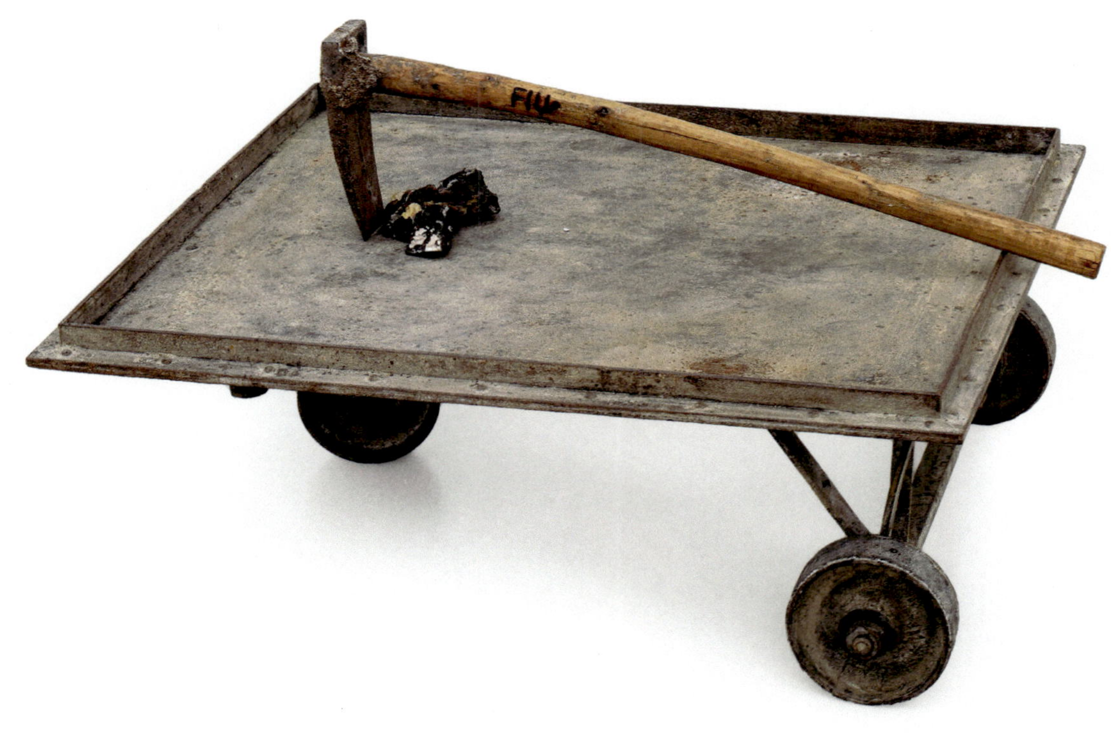

Ziege [Goat], 1958/1982
Three-wheeled cart, iron pick, clay
49 x 93 x 72 cm (19.29 x 36.61 x 28.35 in)

Page 114–115
Hirsch [Stag], 1958/1982

Urtiere [Primordial Animals], 1958/1982
Clay, work tools
Dimensions variable

Page 114
Lehmofen [Clay Oven], 1982

Page 115
Boothia Felix, 1958/1982

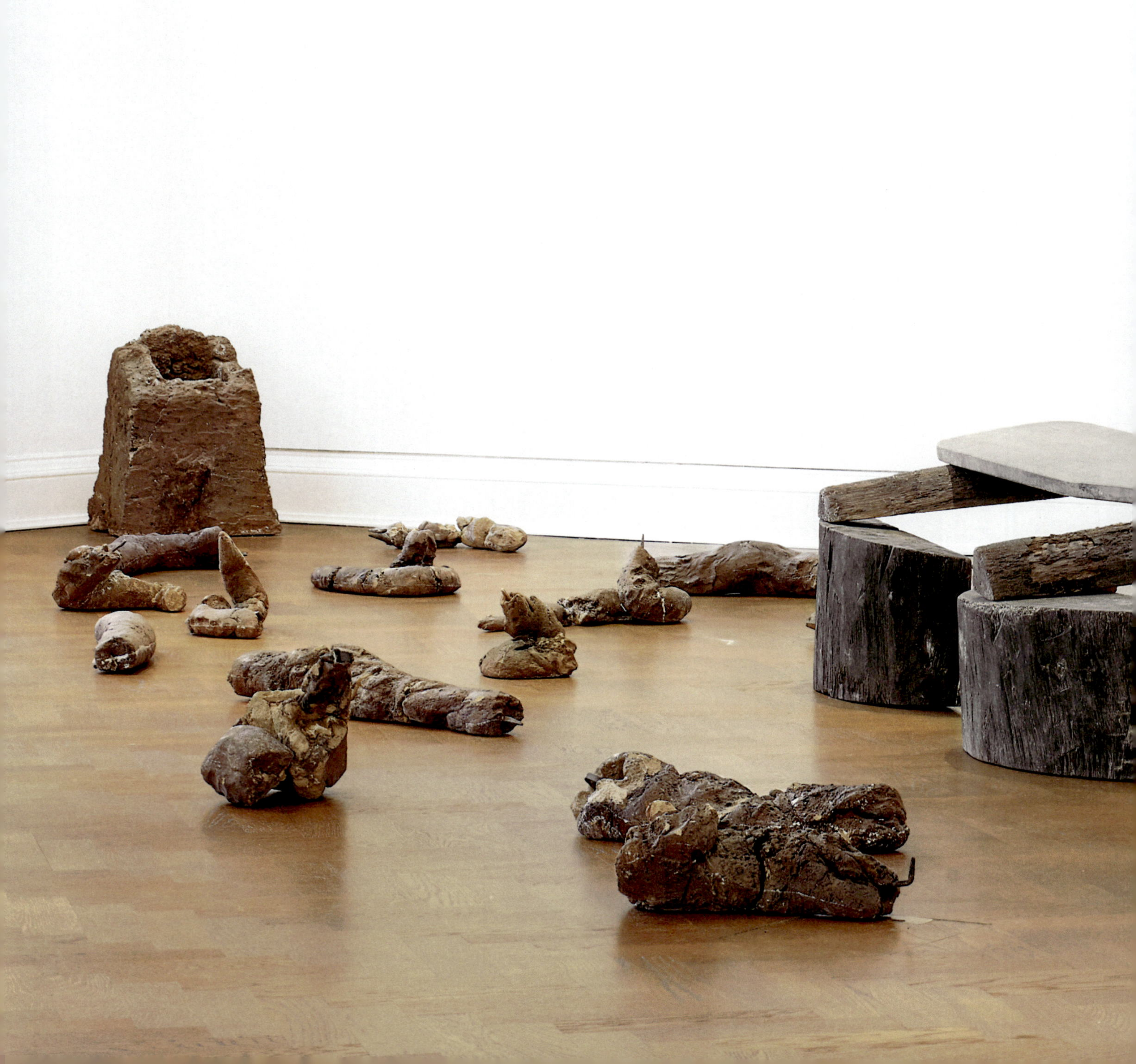

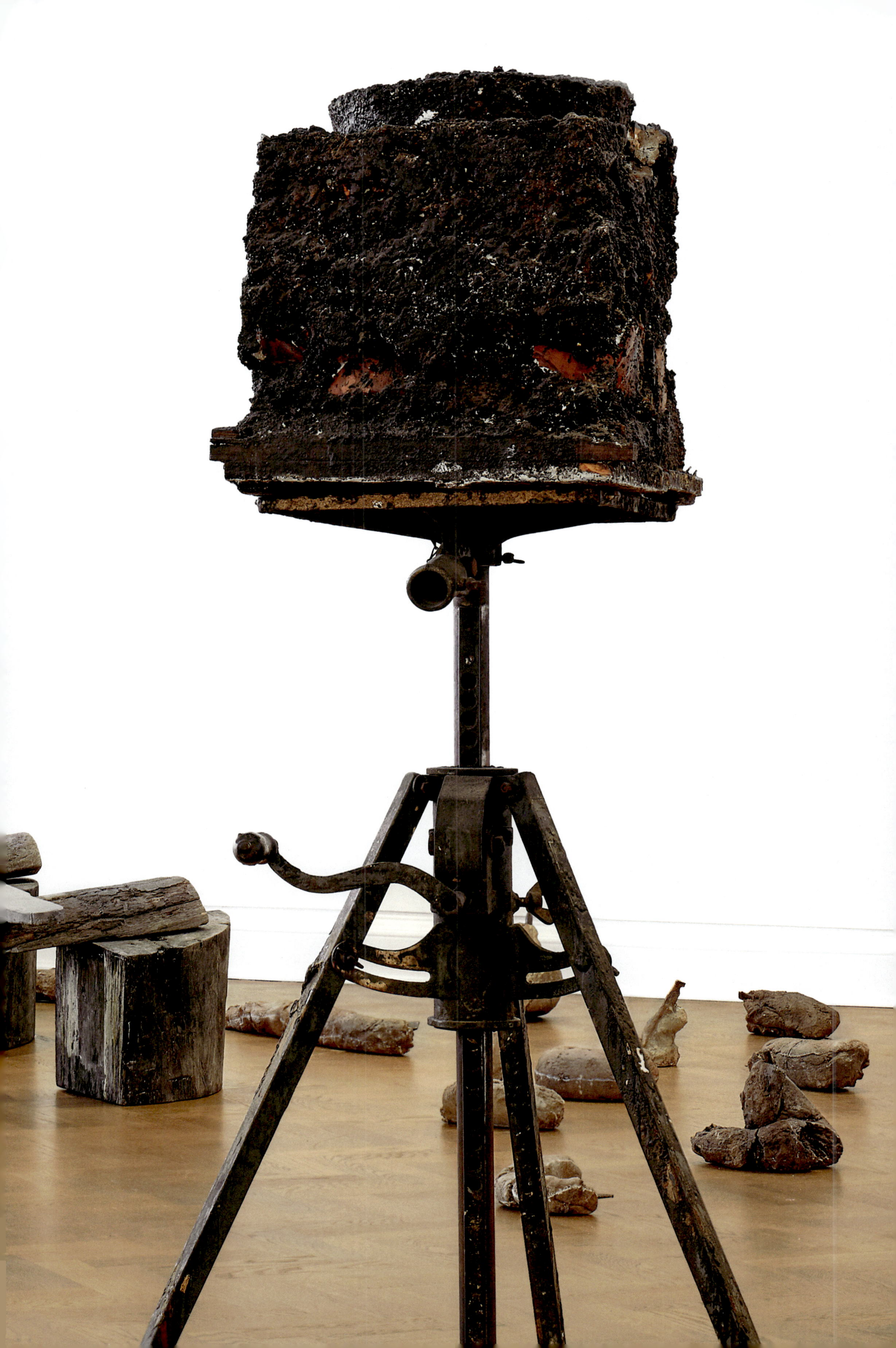

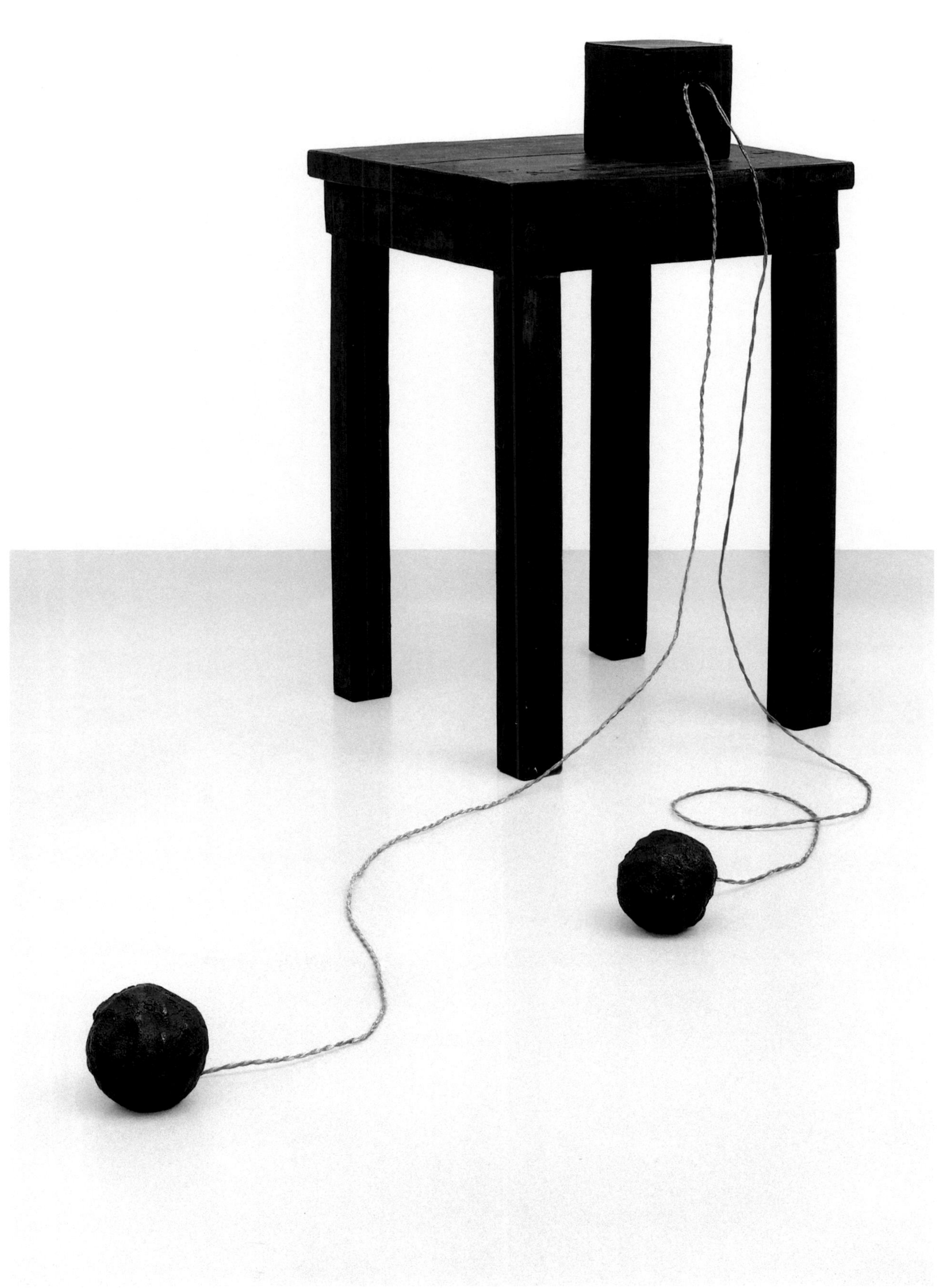

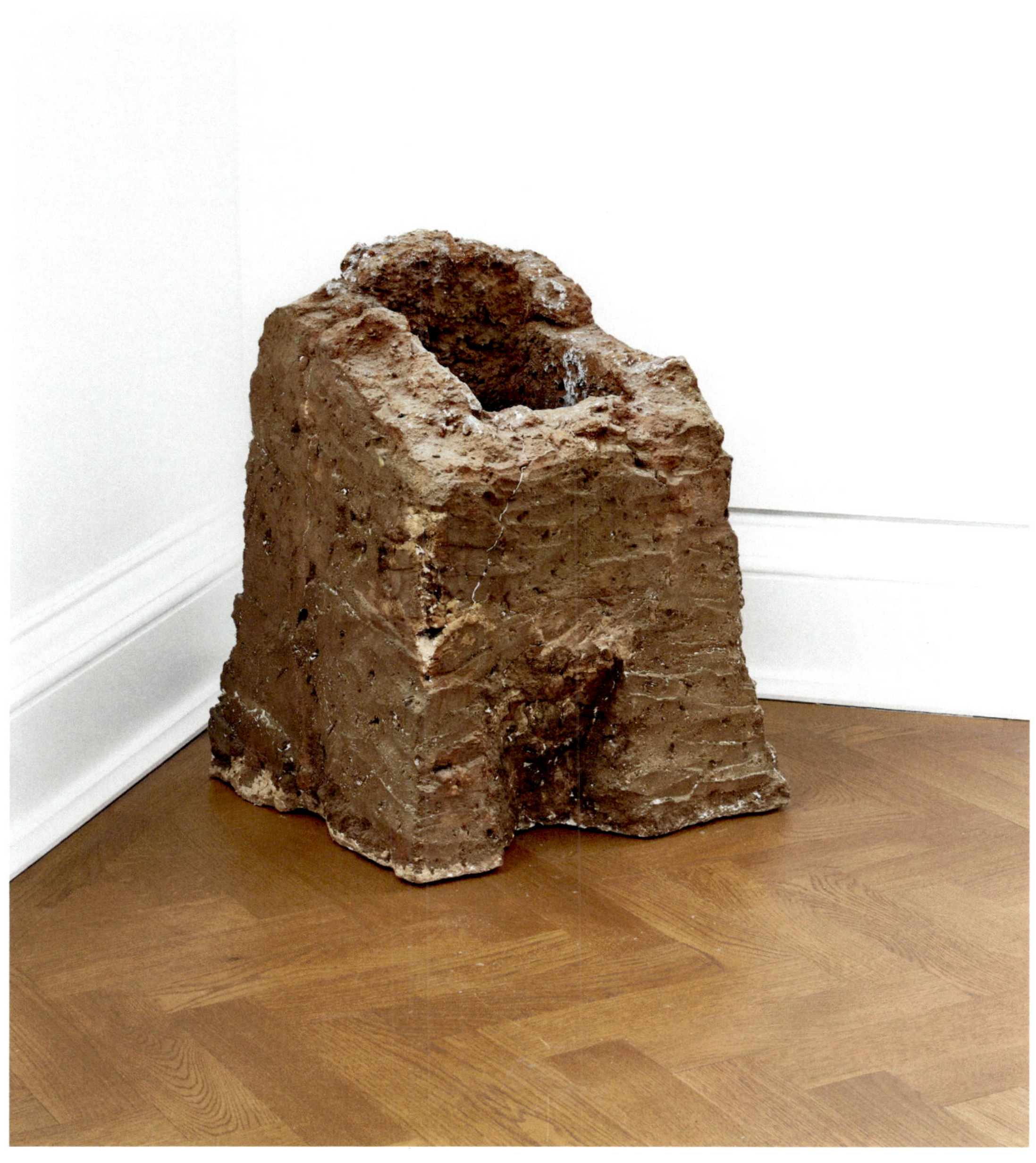

Page 117
Tisch mit Aggregat
[Table with Aggregate], 1958–85
Bronze, wire cables
98.5 x 58 x 170 cm (38.78 x 22.83 x 66.93 in)

Lehmofen [Clay Oven], 1982
Clay, cement mixture
55 x 41 x 41 cm (21.65 x 16.14 x 16.14 in)

DRAWINGS

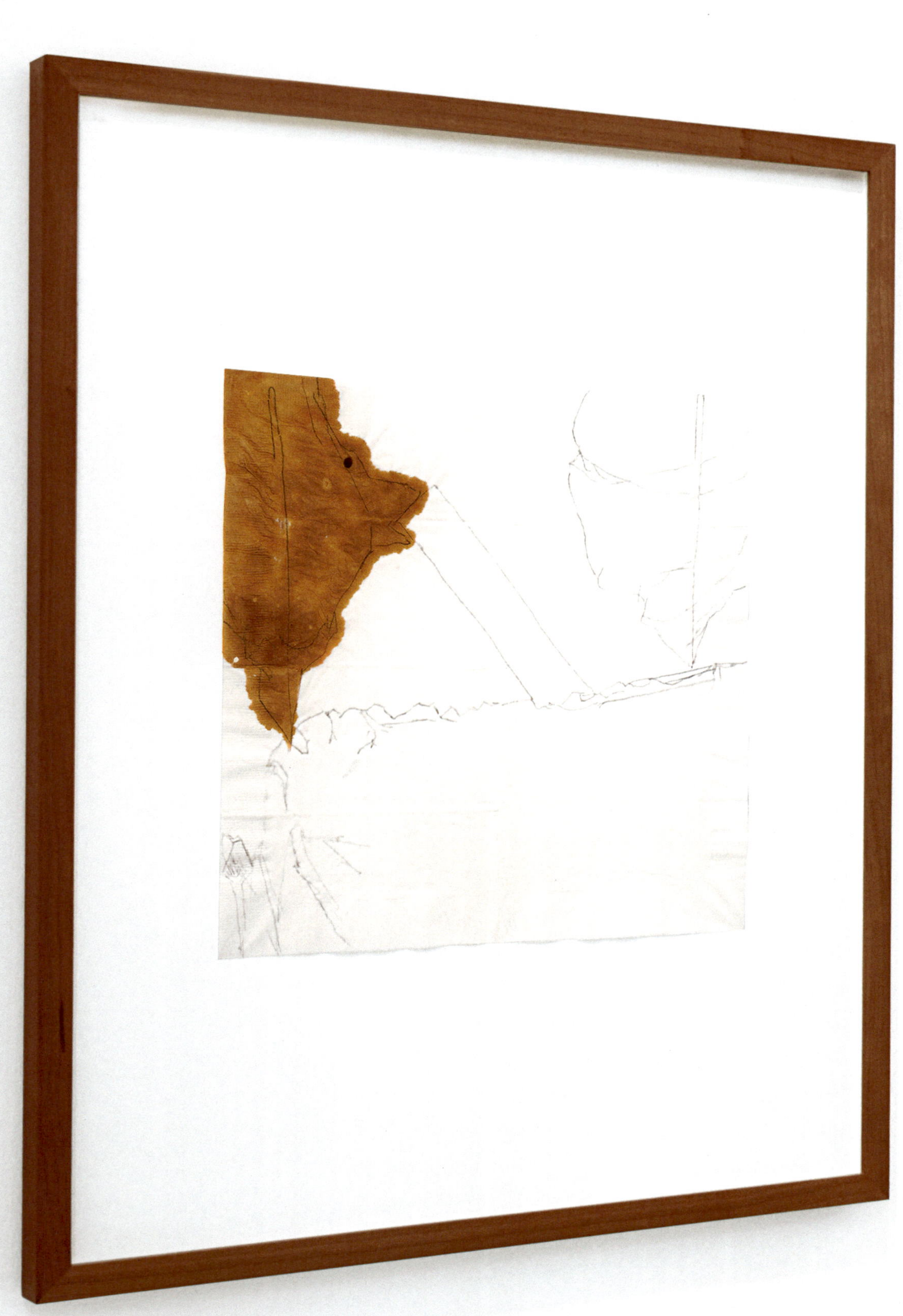

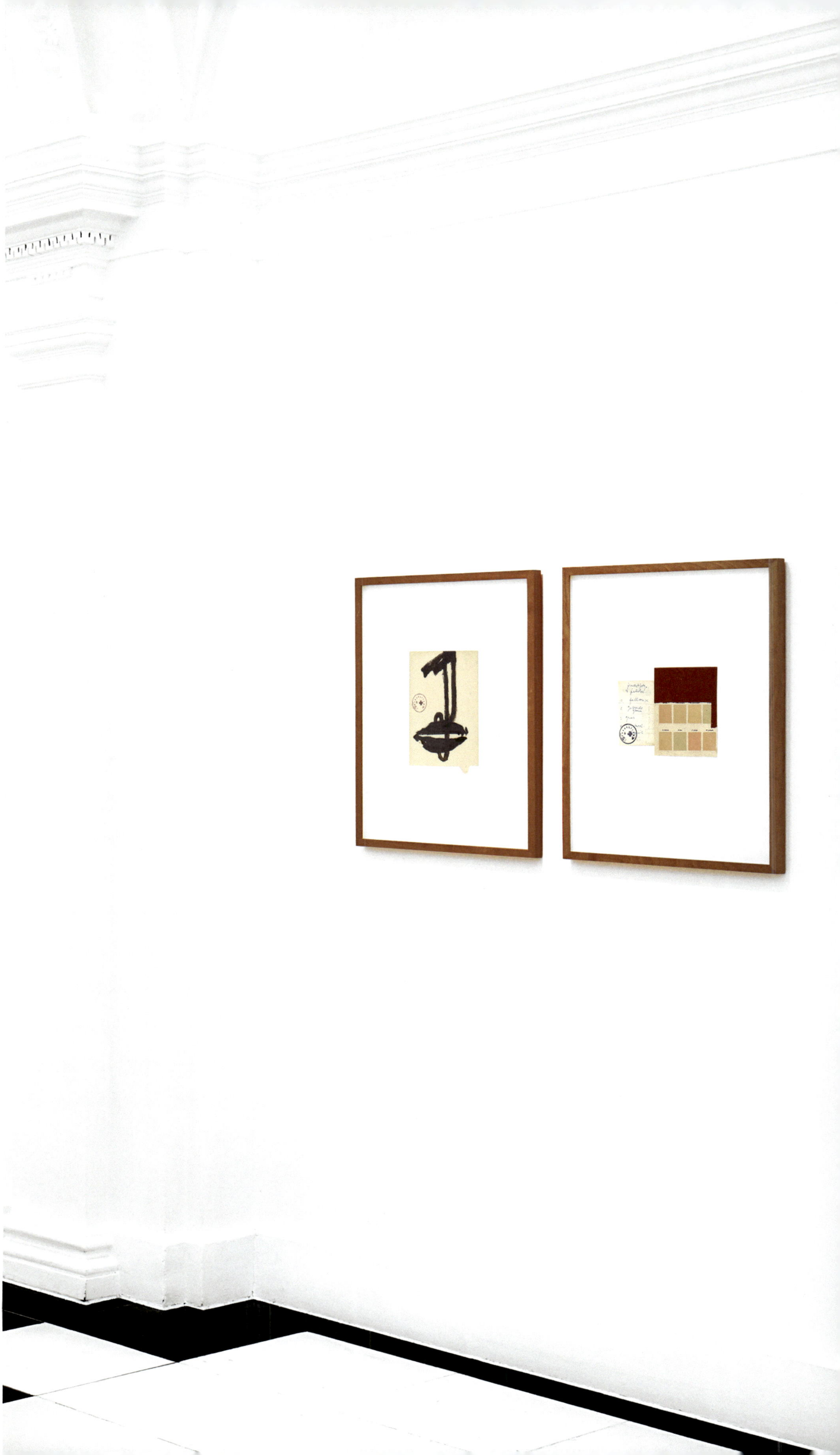

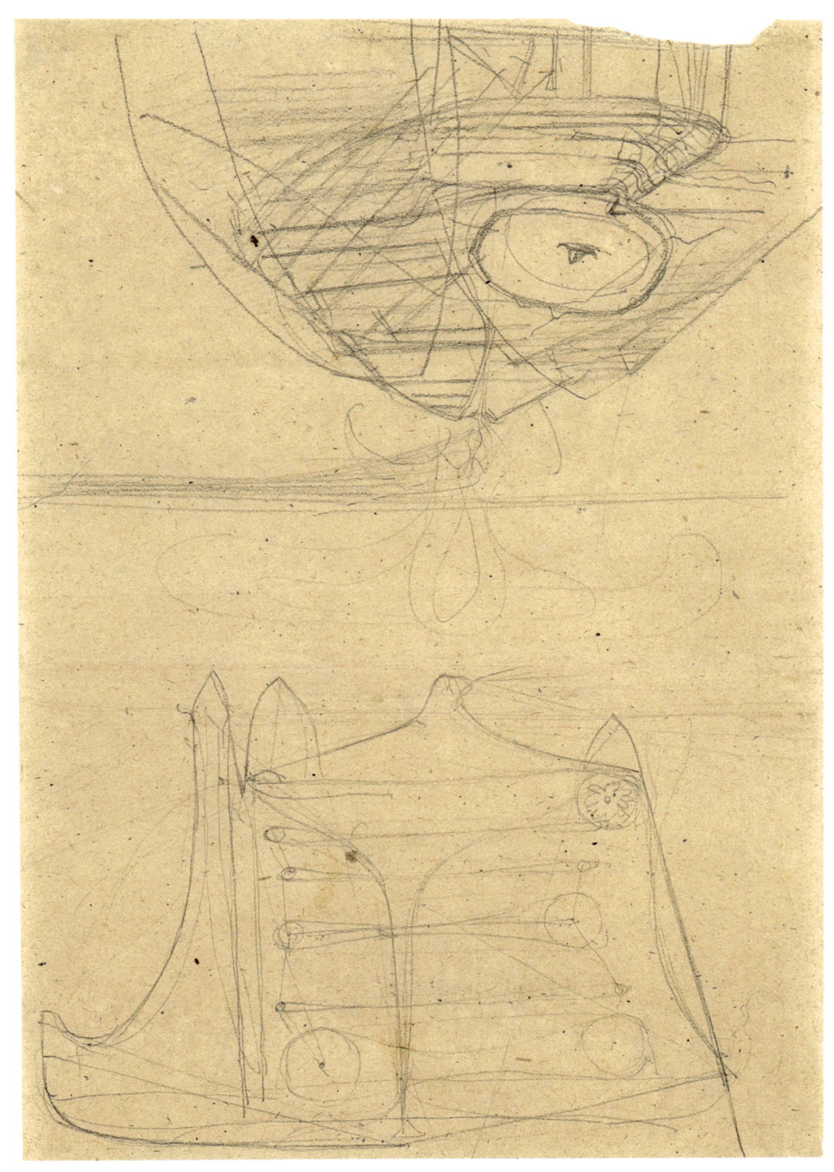

Ohne Titel [Untitled], 1947
Pencil on silk paper
29.5 x 21 cm (11.62 x 8.27 in)

Frau D.B. [Mrs D.B.], 1955
Pencil on paper
29.5 x 21 cm (11.61 x 8.27 in)

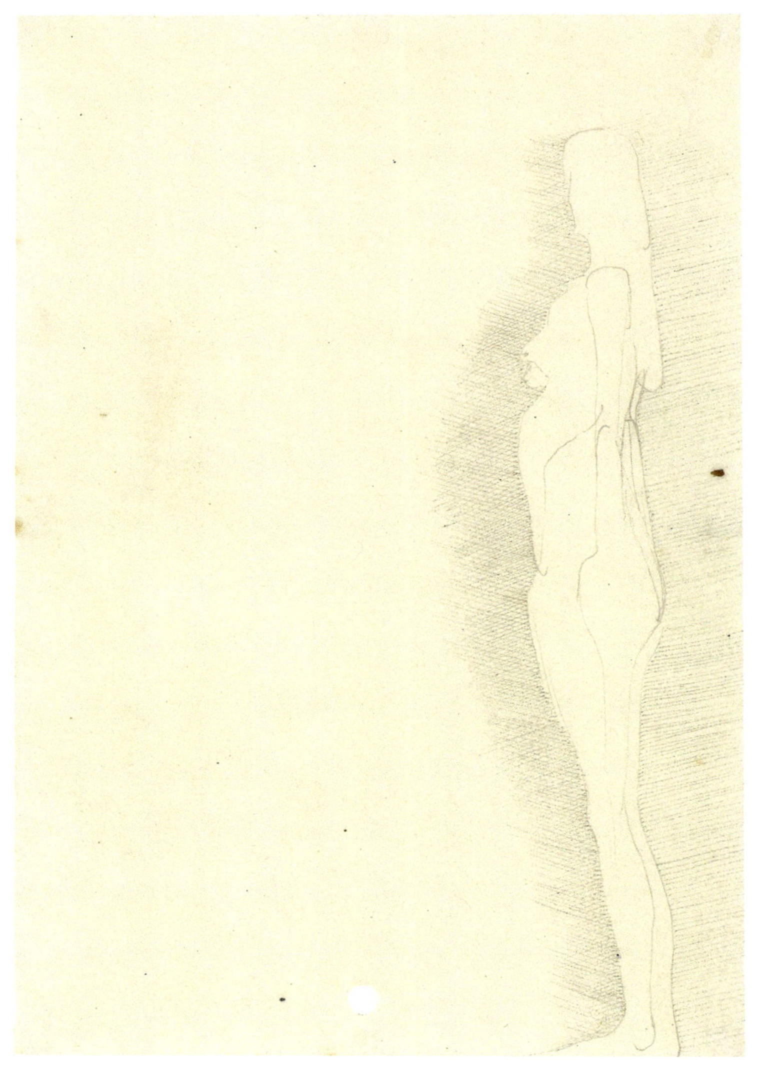

Stehende Weibliche Figur
[Standing Female Figure], 1951
Pencil on tissue paper
20.3 x 14.3 cm (7.99 x 5.63 in)

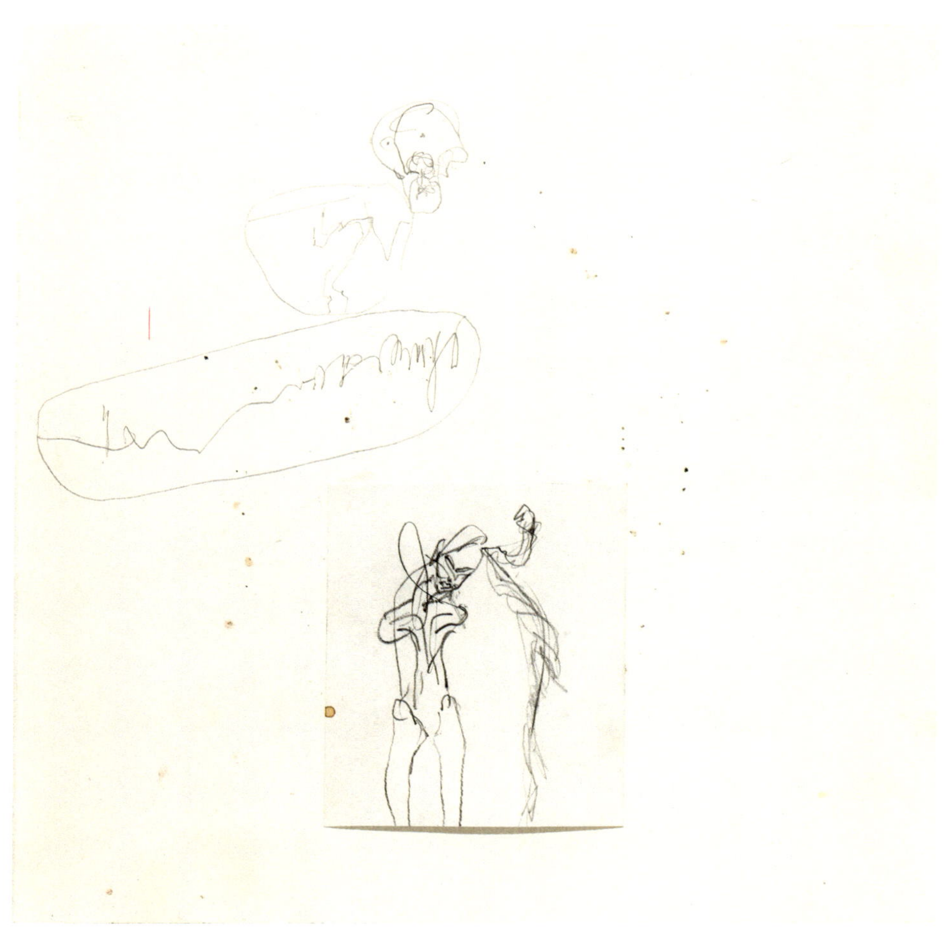

Der Tod und das Mädchen
[Death and the Girl], 1955/1958
Pencil and paper collaged on paper
25.2 x 25.9 cm (9.92 x 10.2 in)

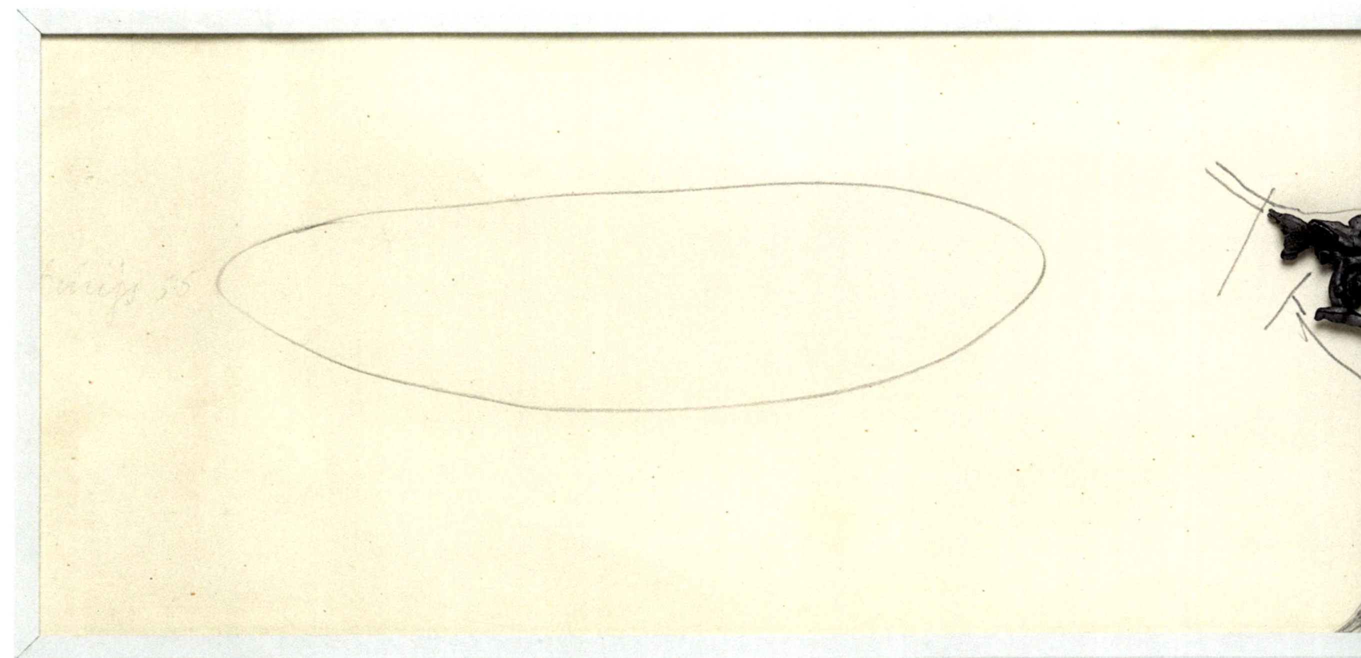

Ohne Titel [Untitled], 1955
Metal, fat and graphite on paper
15.6 x 70.5 cm (6.14 x 27.76 in)

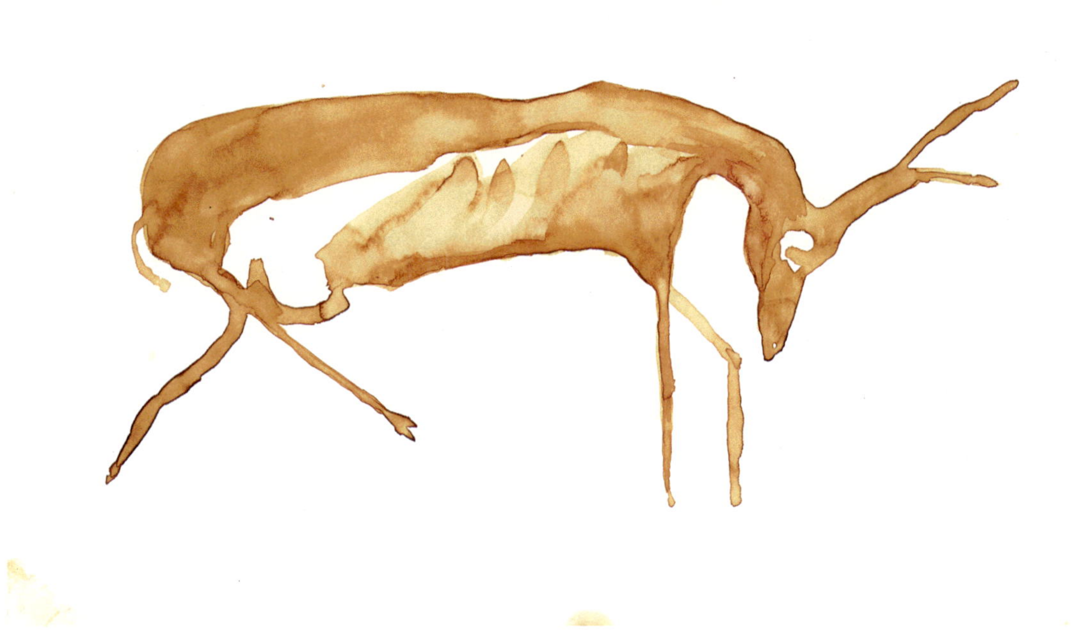

Hirsch [Stag], 1956
Watercolour on paper
19 x 28 cm (7.48 x 11.02 in)

Hirschdenkmal
[Monument to the Stag], 1958
Pencil and moss rubbed on paper
22.9 x 33 cm (9 x 13 in)

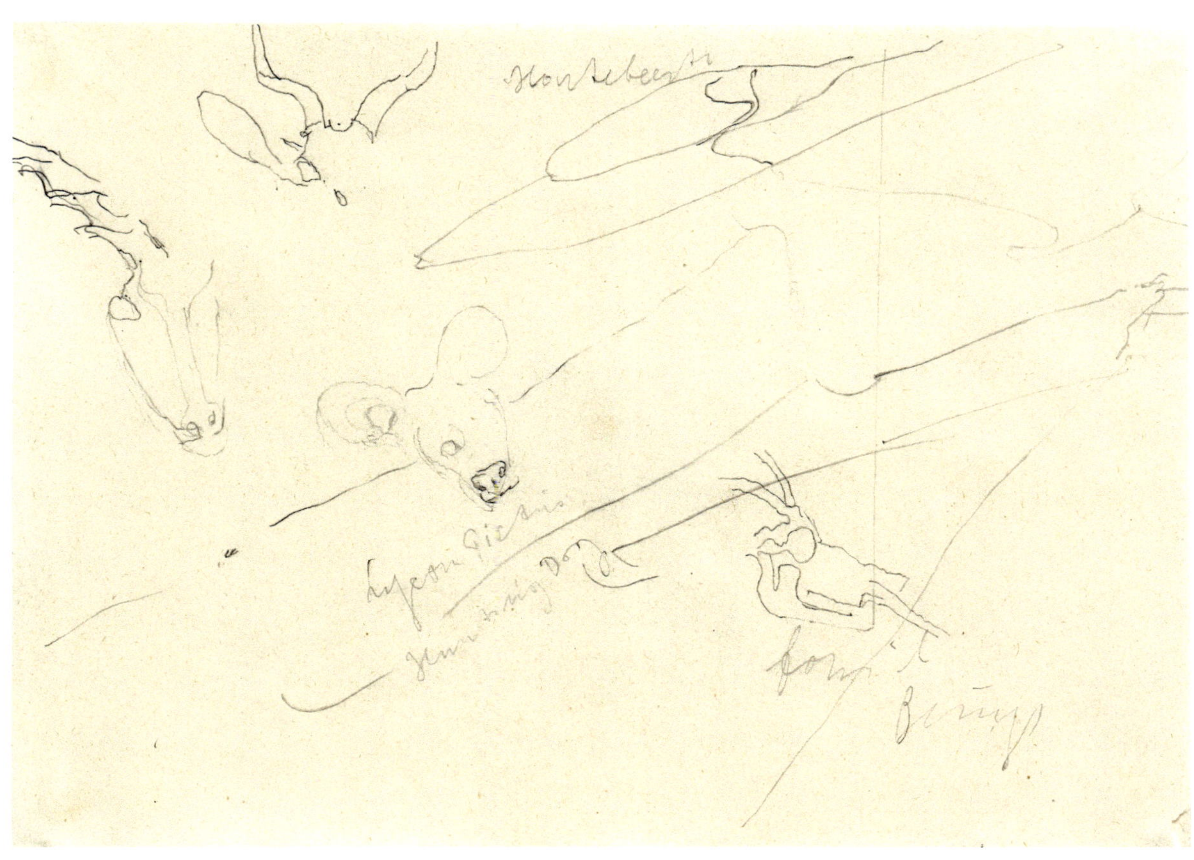

Lycaon Pictus, Hunting Dog, 1974
Pencil on vellum
20.8 x 30 cm (8.19 x 11.81 in)

Hirschkuh [Hind], 1972
Pencil on paper
66.5 x 50 cm (26.18 x 19.69 in)

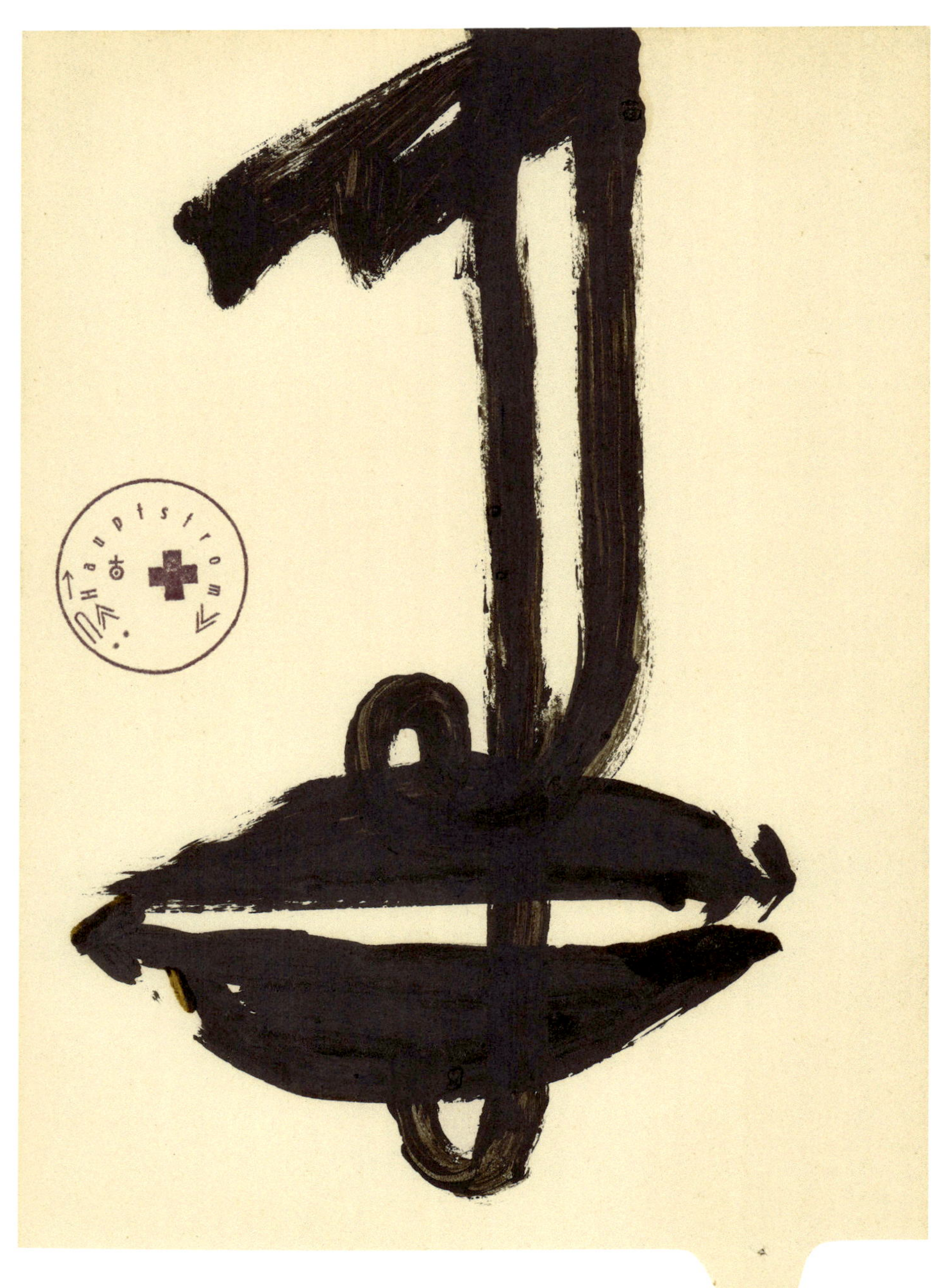

Ohne Titel [Untitled], 1960
Grey oil with 'Hauptstrom'
[Mainstream] stamp on card
29.2 x 20.6 cm (11.5 x 8.11 in)

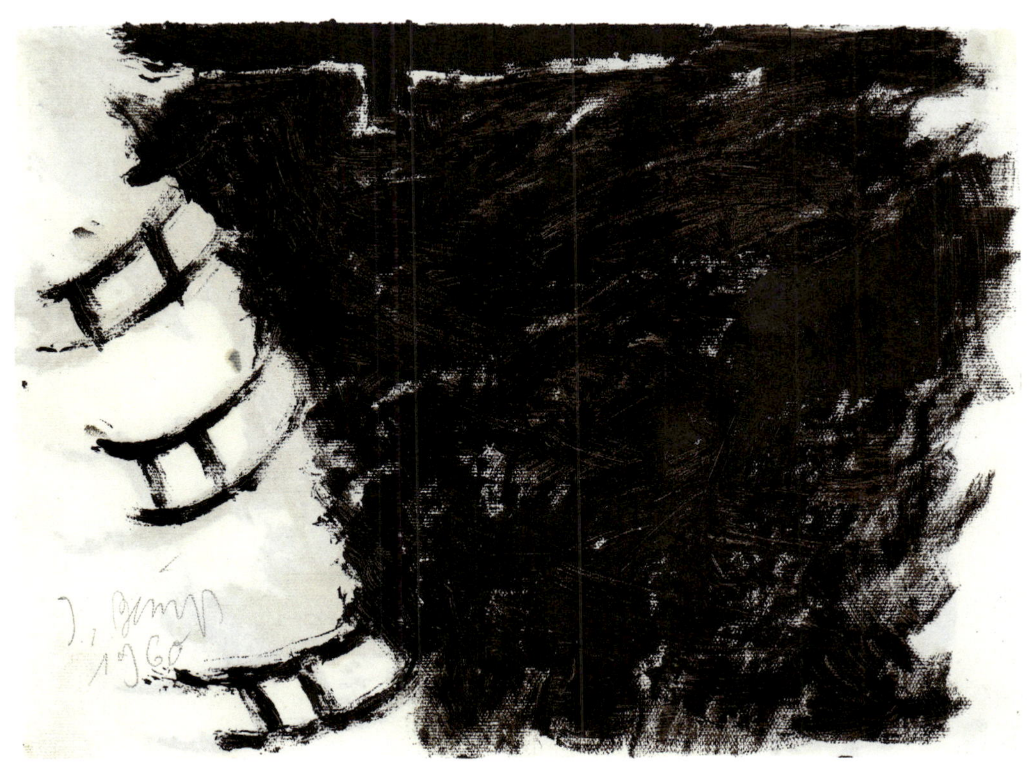

Schlitten [Sleds], 1960
Pencil and grey oil on paper
15 x 21 cm (5.91 x 8.27 in)

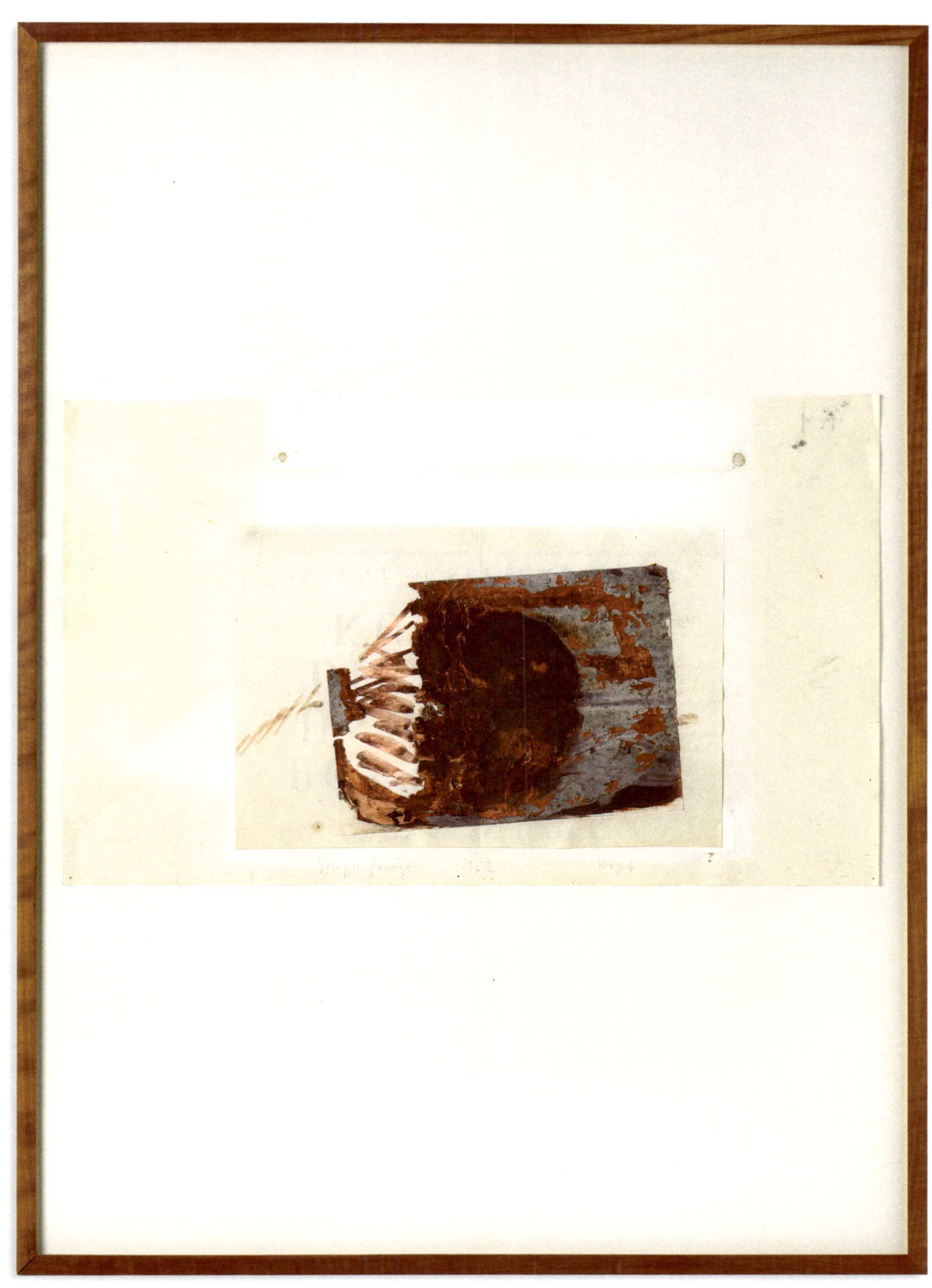

Kopf [Head], 1962
Paint and printed-paper collage on paper
41 x 70 cm (16.14 x 27.56 in)
Framed: 107 x 78.5 x 3.2 cm
(42.13 x 30.91 x 1.26 in)

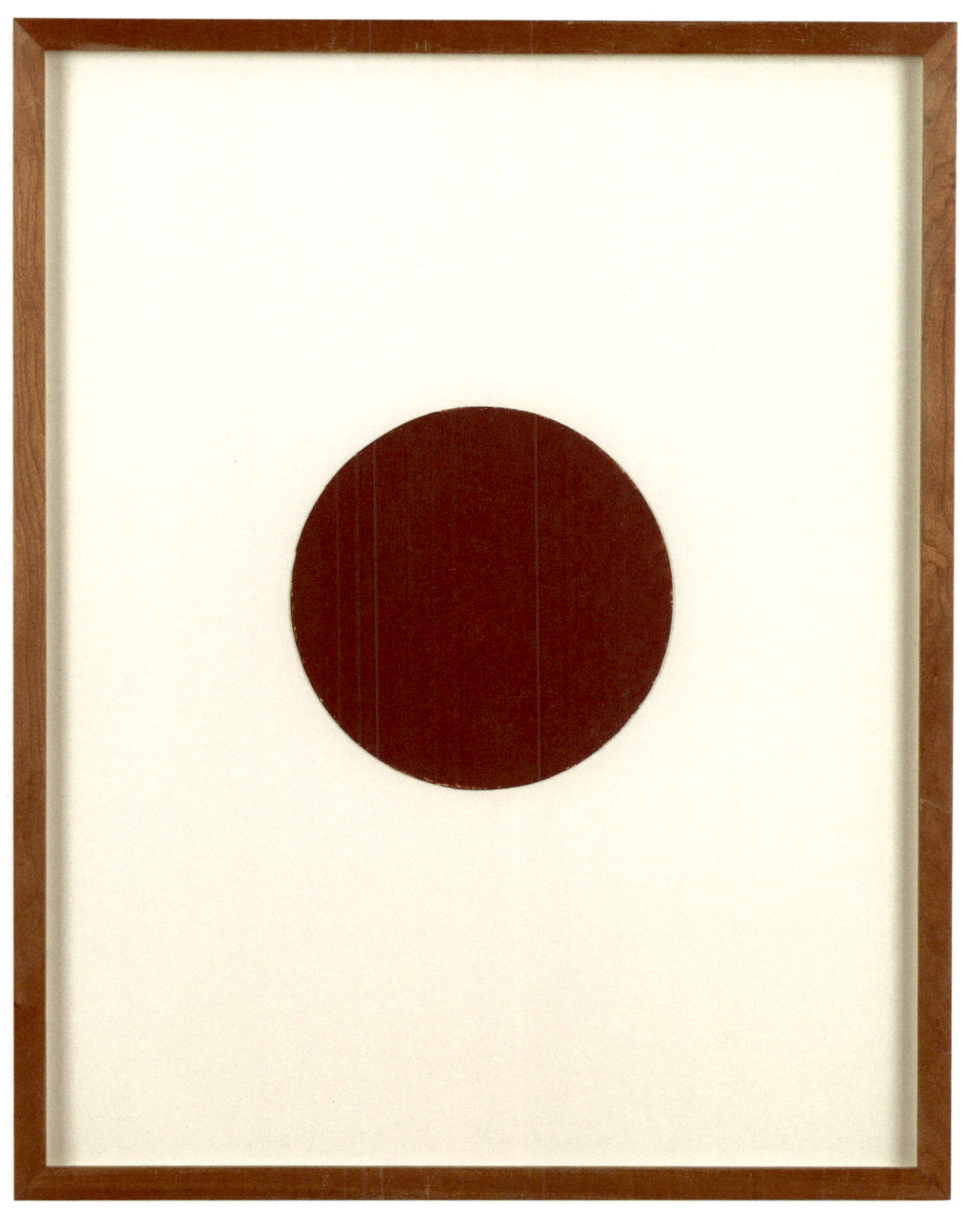

Braunkreuz, 1964
Oil and fat (Braunkreuz) on prepared card
Ø 21.6 cm (Ø 8.5 in)
Framed: 64.8 x 51.4 cm (25.51 x 20.24 in)

Braunkreuz, 1966–67
Oil (Braunkreuz) on newspaper, two parts
Upper part: 27.2 x 40.5 cm (10.71 x 15.94 in)
Lower part: 30.5 x 42 cm (12.01 x 16.54 in)

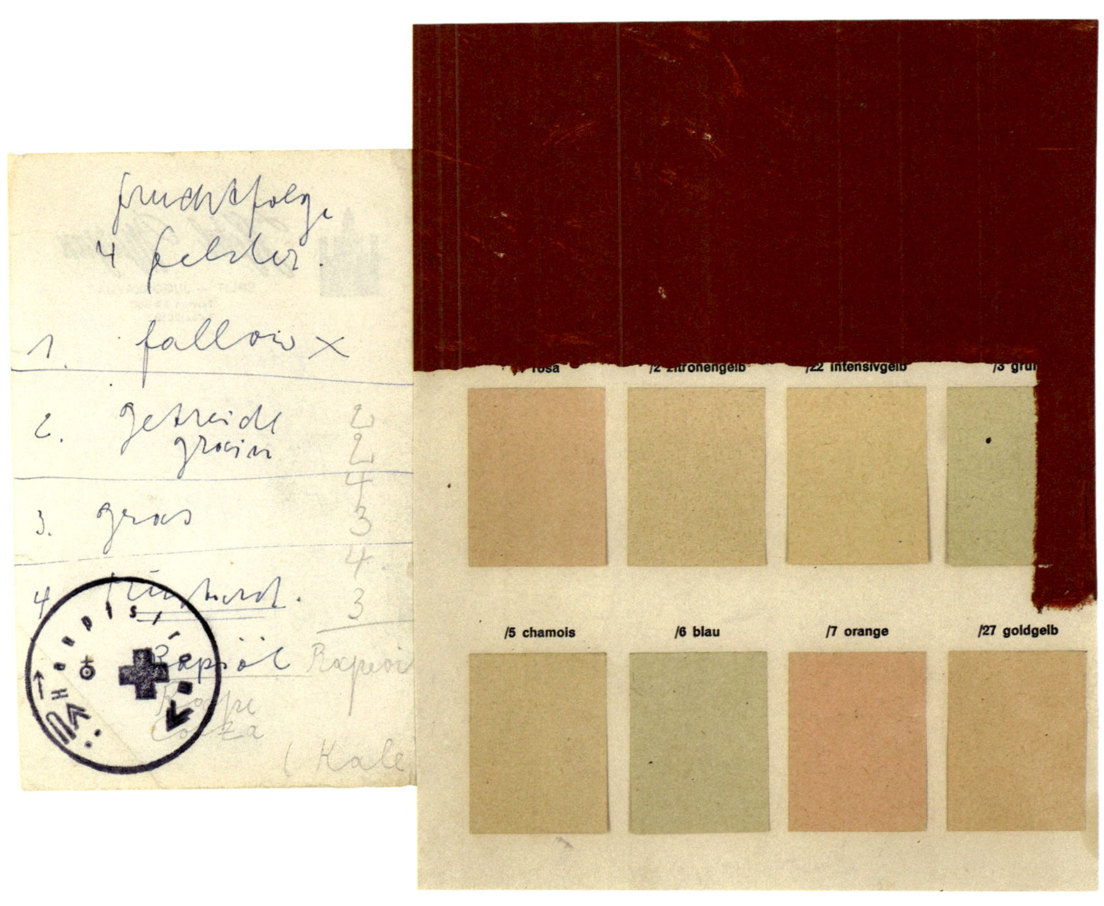

Runrig, 1973
Collage with pencil, pen and ink,
oil (Braunkreuz) and 'Hauptstrom'
[Mainstream] stamp on paper
19.7 x 24.4 cm (7.76 x 9.61 in)

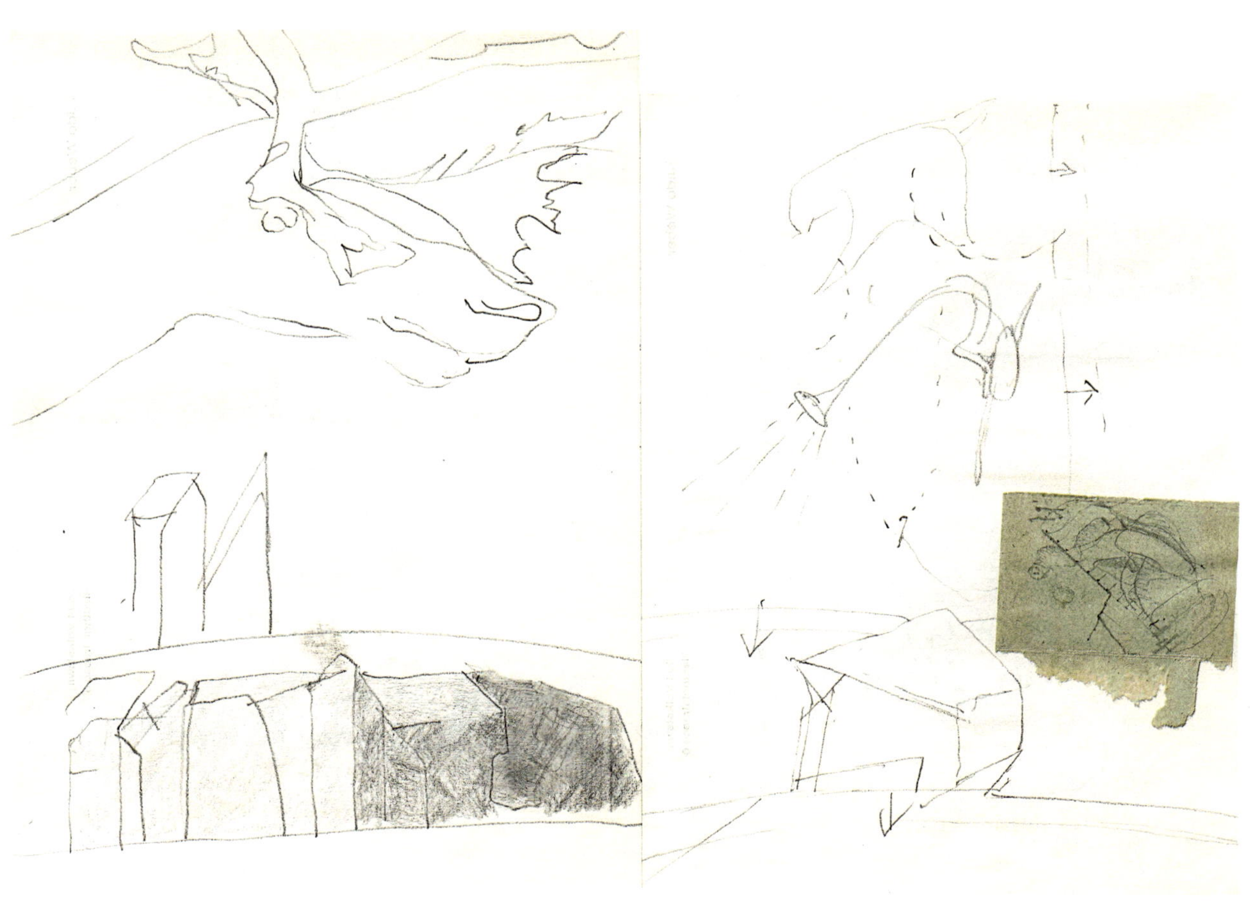

Sternbild des Bären / junger Elch rechts über dem Haus des alten Müllers
[Constellation of the Bear / Young Elk Right Over the Old Miller's House], 1961–63
Pencil on paper
20.2 x 29 cm (7.95 x 11.42 in)

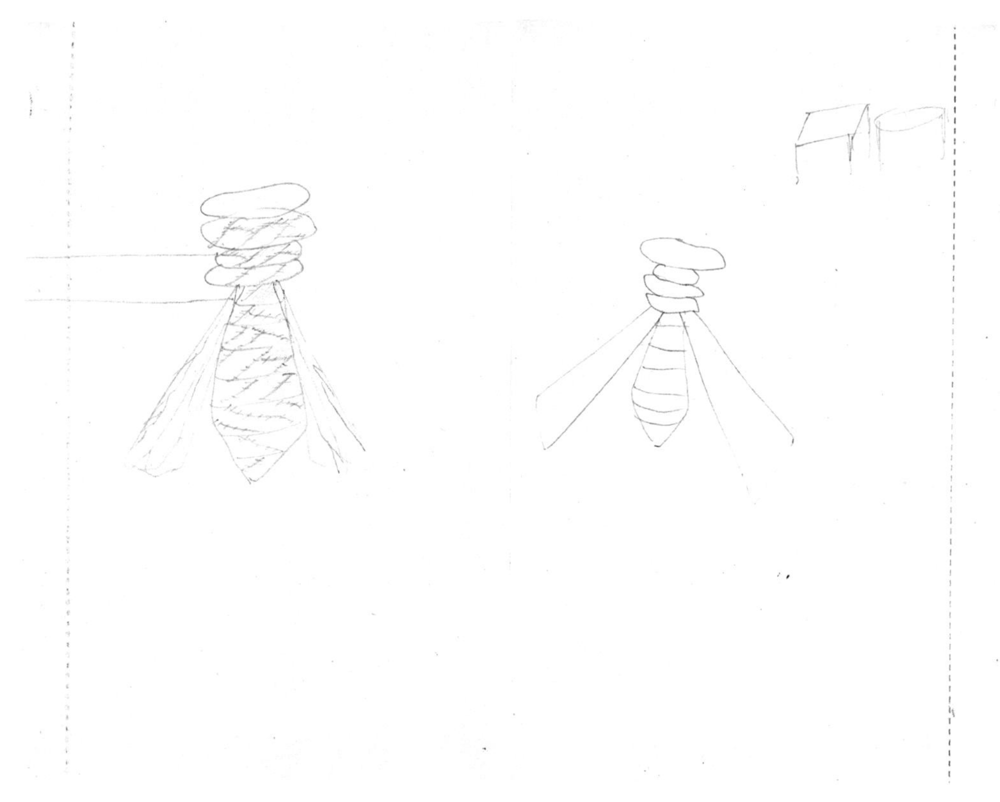

Biene [Bee], 1970
Pencil on paper, two parts
Each: 21.5 x 13.5 cm
(8.46 x 5.31 in)

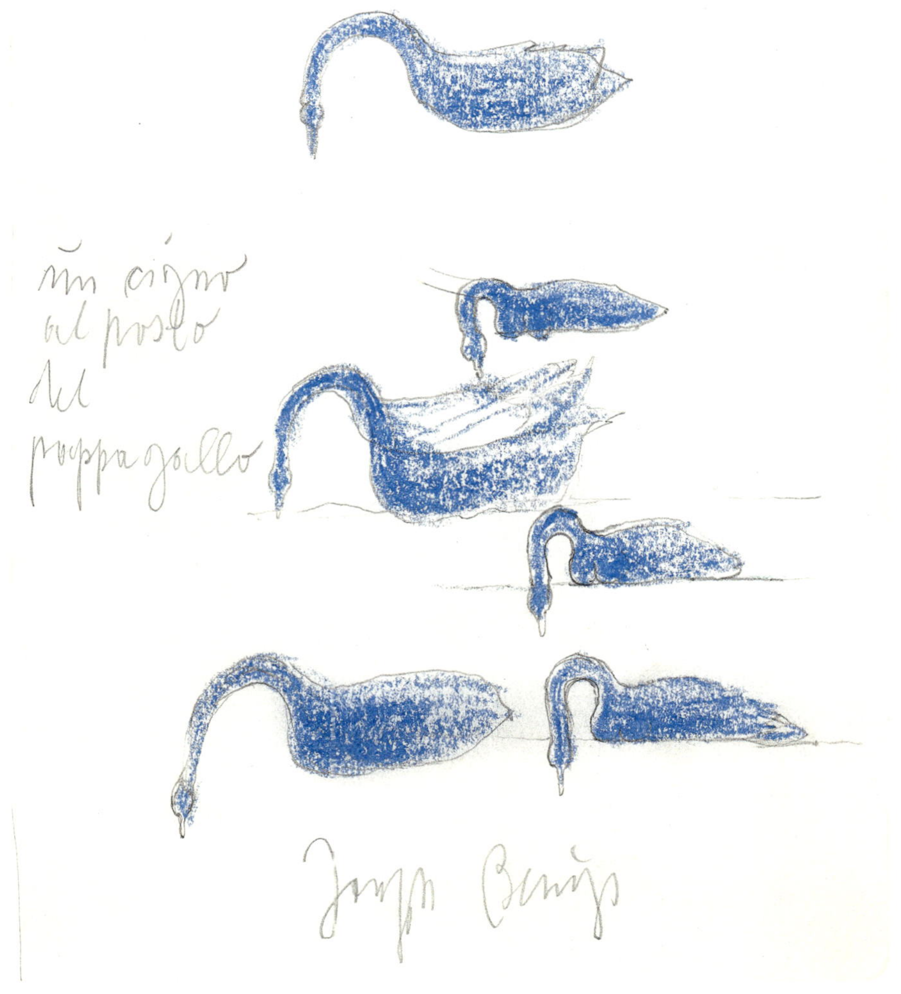

Schwäne [Swans], 1981–82
Pencil and blue pastel on paper
23 x 16.5 cm (9.06 x 6.5 in)

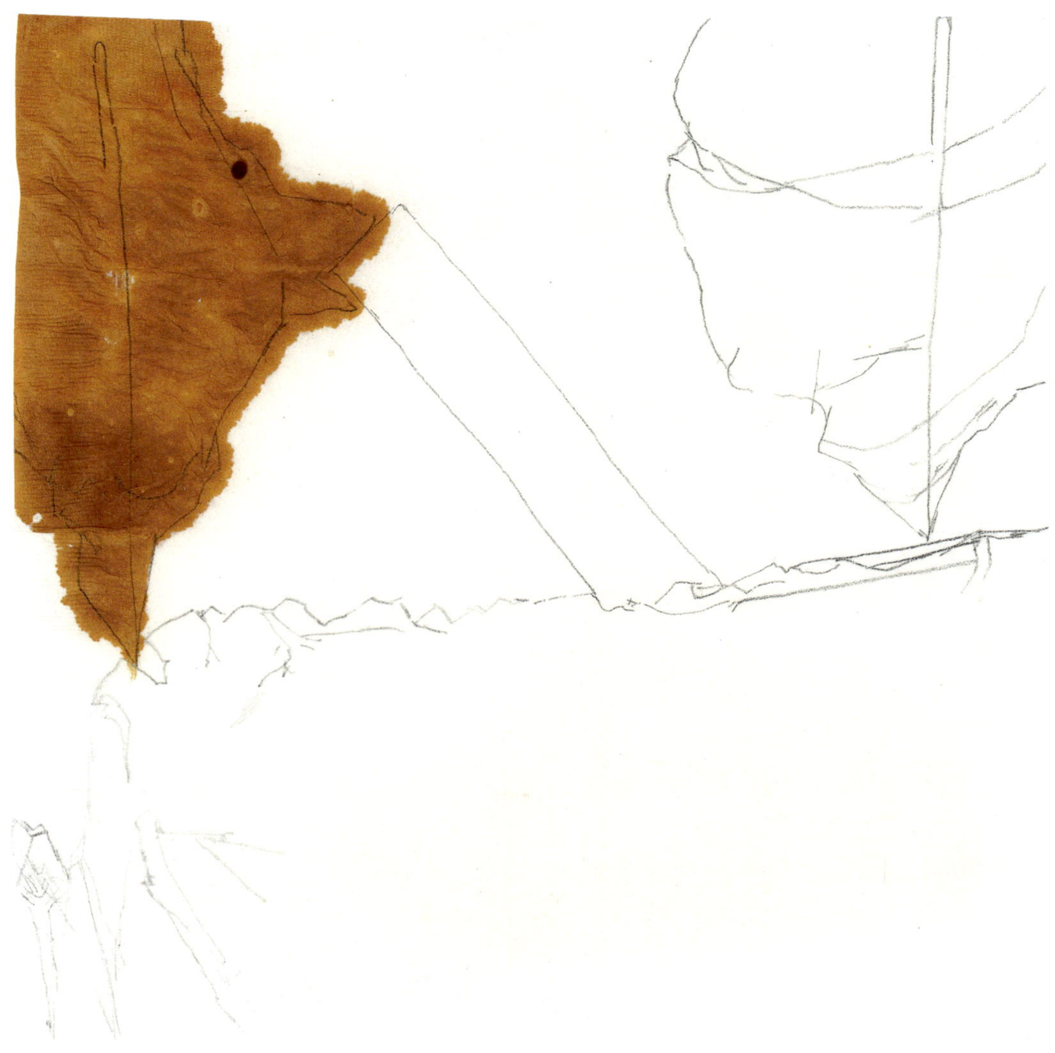

Das Wetter in den Bergen von Wien
[The Weather in the Mountains from Vienna], 1980
Pencil and pigment on paper
33 x 33 cm (12.99 x 12.99 in)

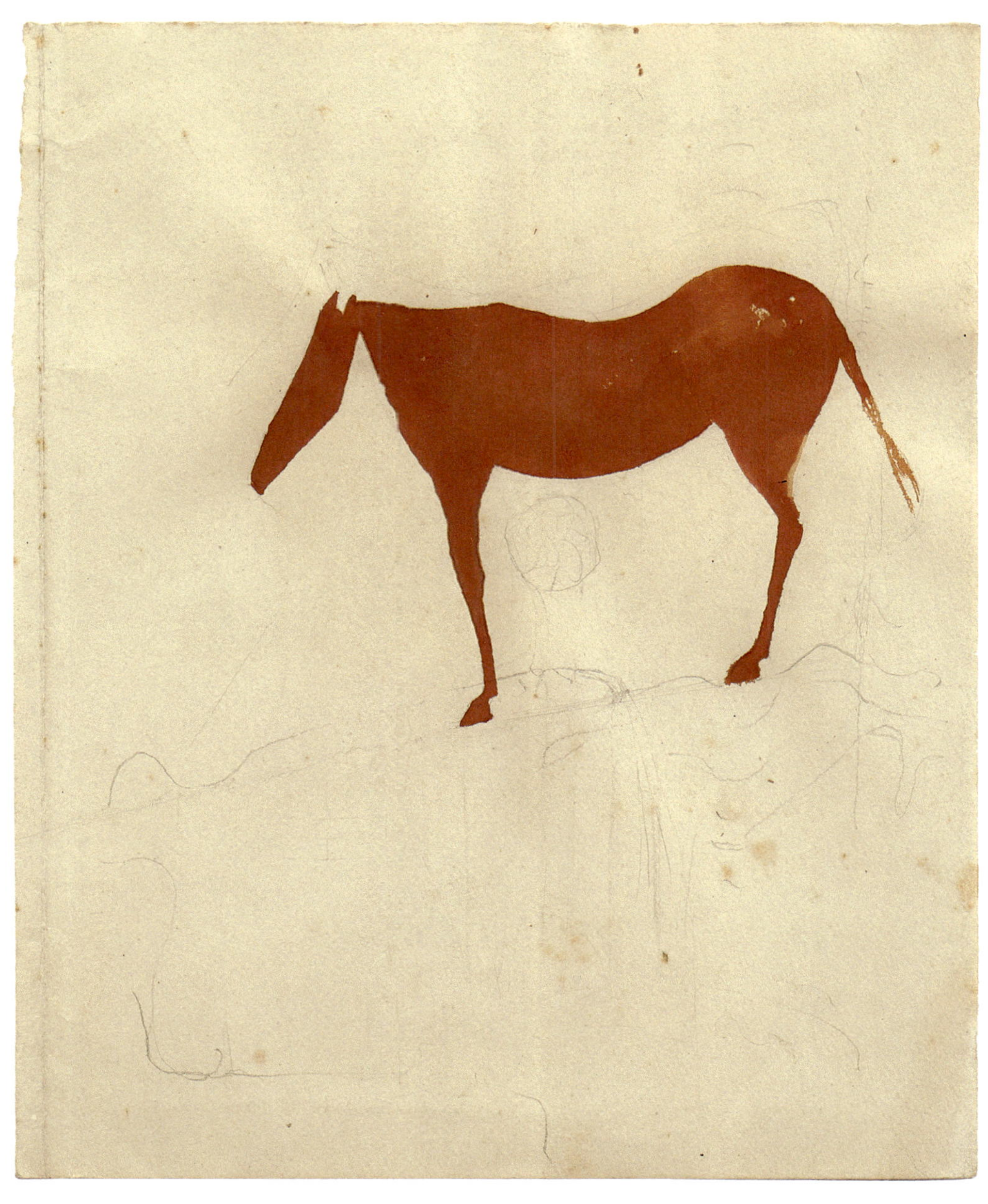

Ohne Titel [Untitled], undated
Pencil and pigment on paper
24.6 x 20.8 cm (9.69 x 8.19 in)

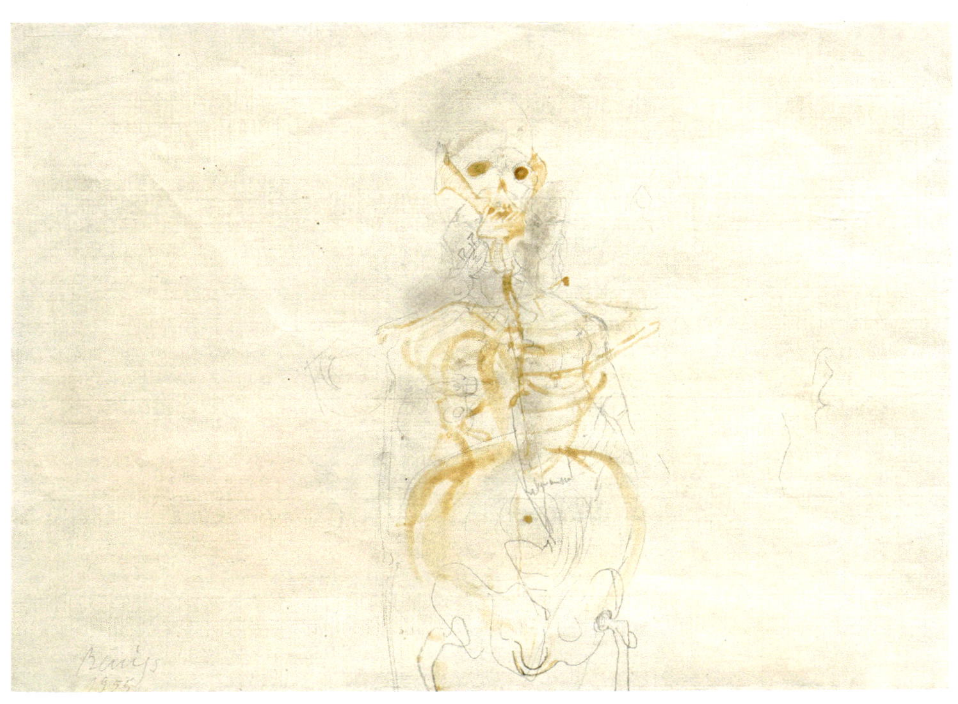

Ohne Titel [Untitled], 1955
Pencil and watercolour on paper, two-sided
21 x 29.7 cm (8.27 x 11.69 in)

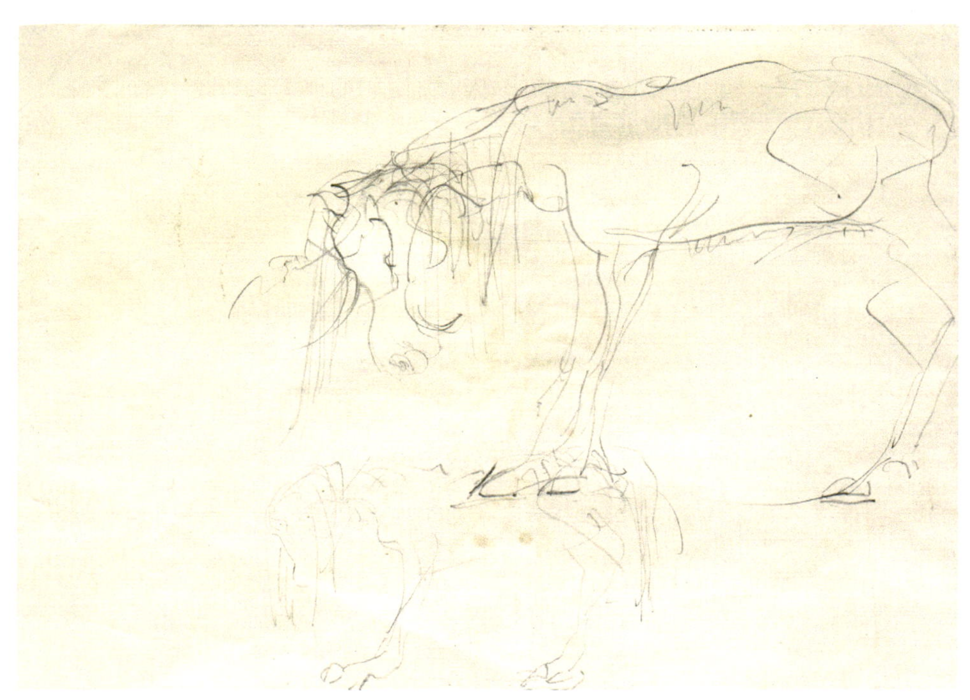

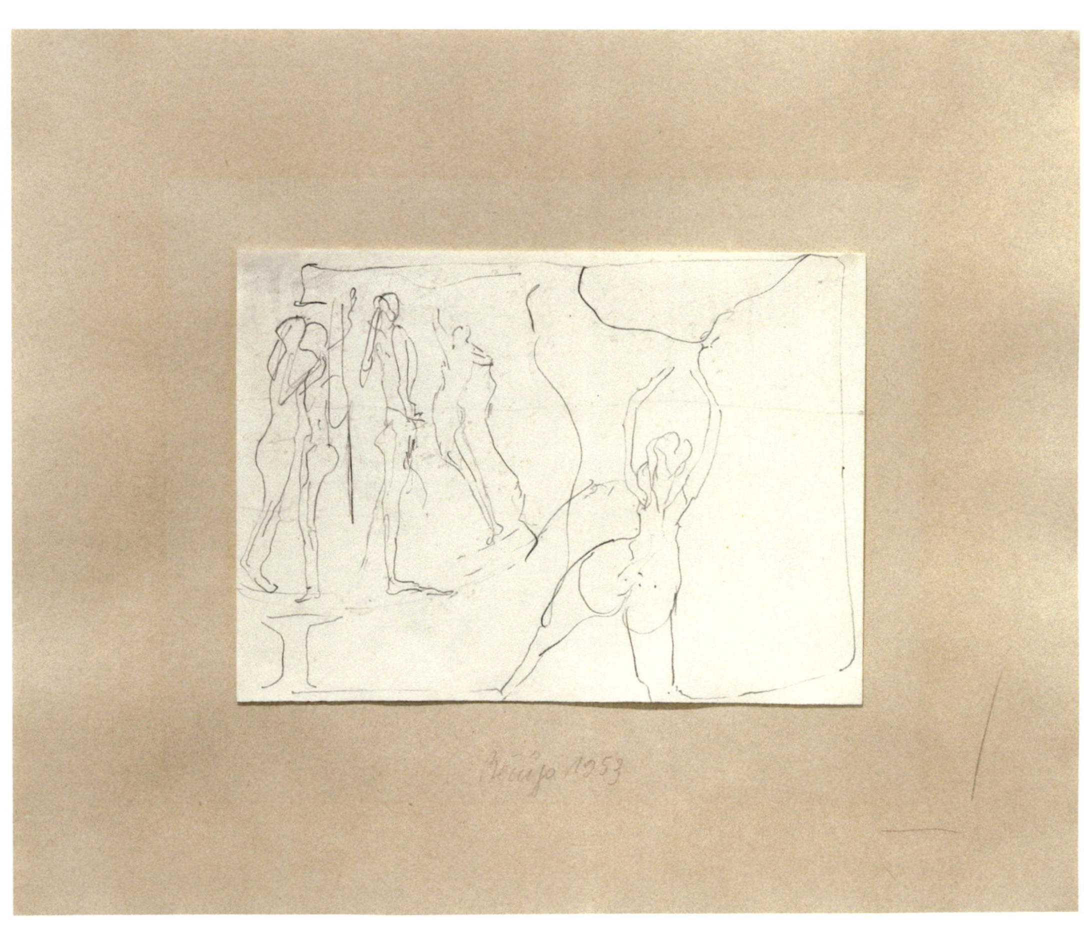

Ohne Titel [Untitled], 1953
Pencil on paper mounted on backing paper
29 x 35 cm (11.42 x 13.78 in)

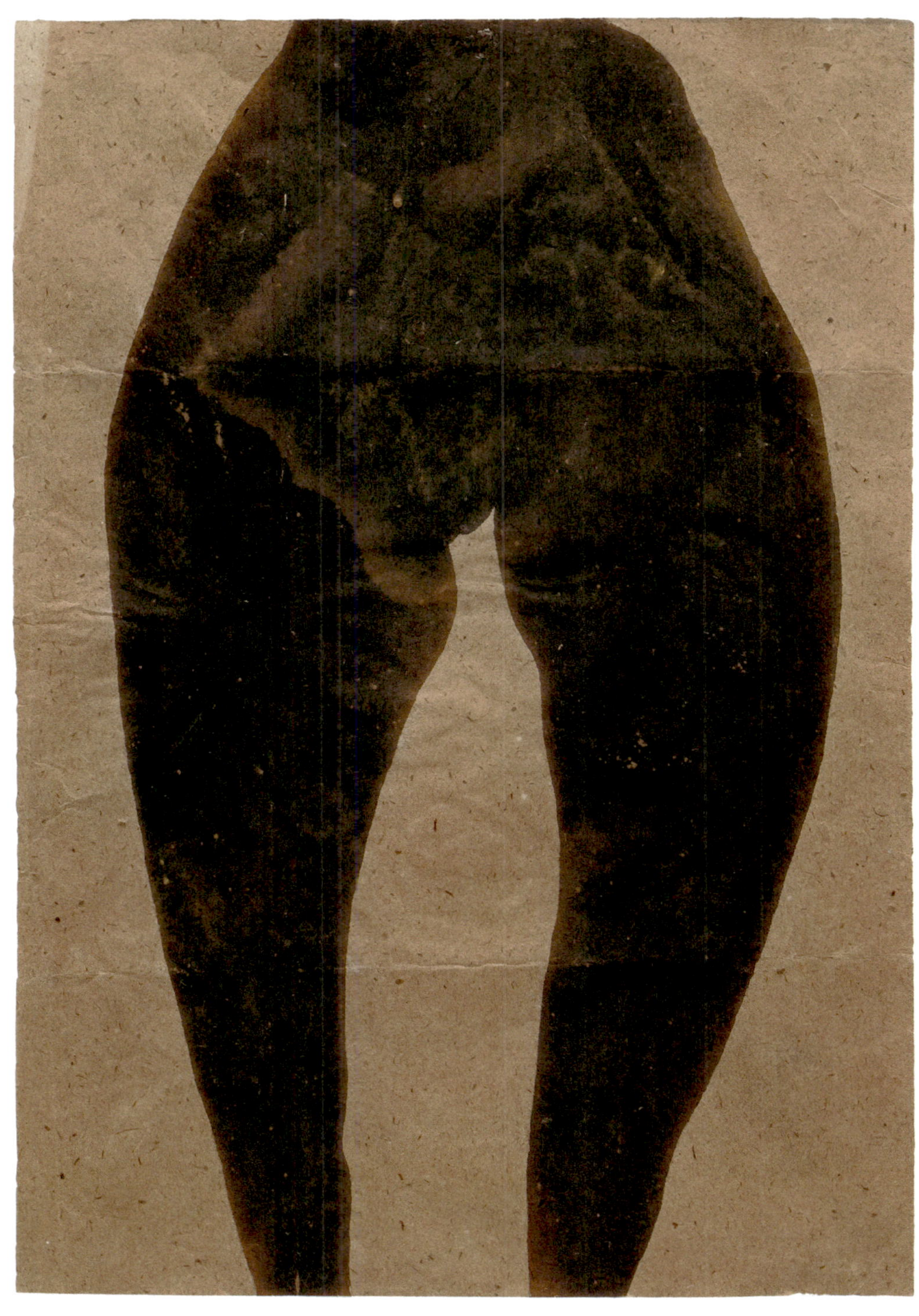

Ohne Titel [Untitled], 1954
Watercolour on brown paper
35 x 24.5 cm (13.78 x 9.65 in)

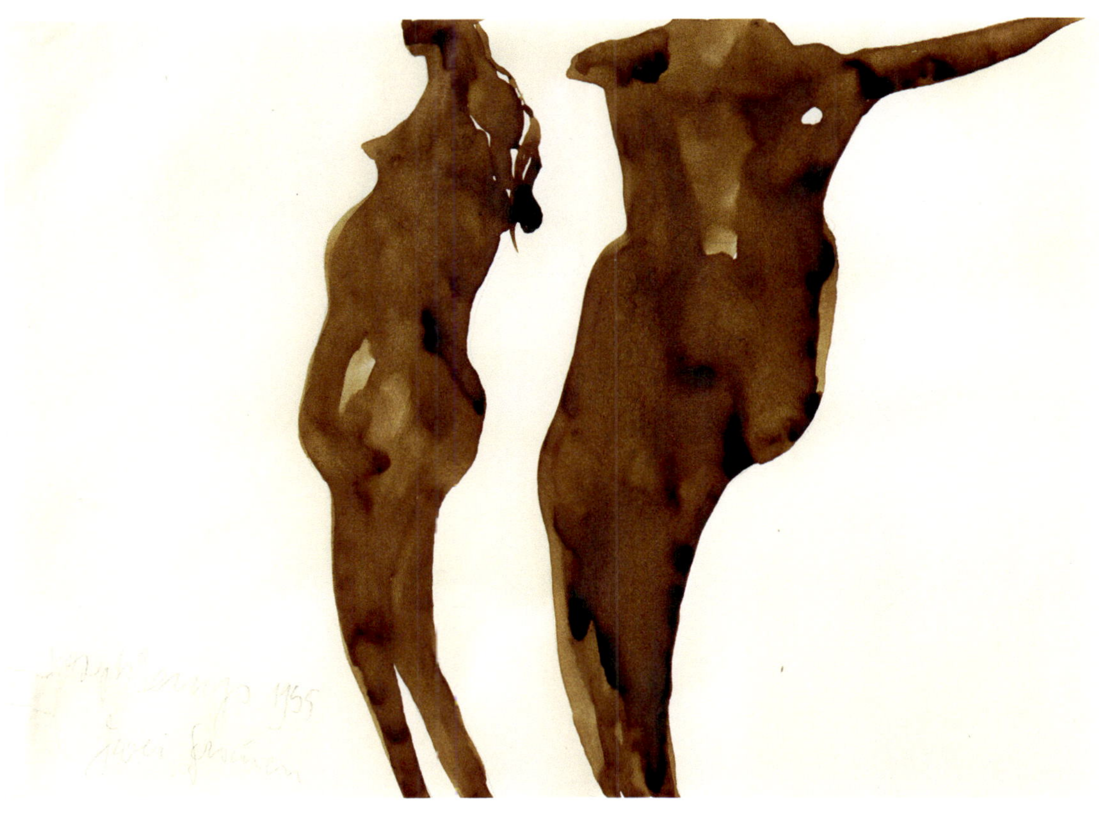

Zwei Frauen [Two Women], 1955
Pencil, watercolour, gouache
and iron chloride on paper
21 x 29.5 cm (8.27 x 11.61 in)

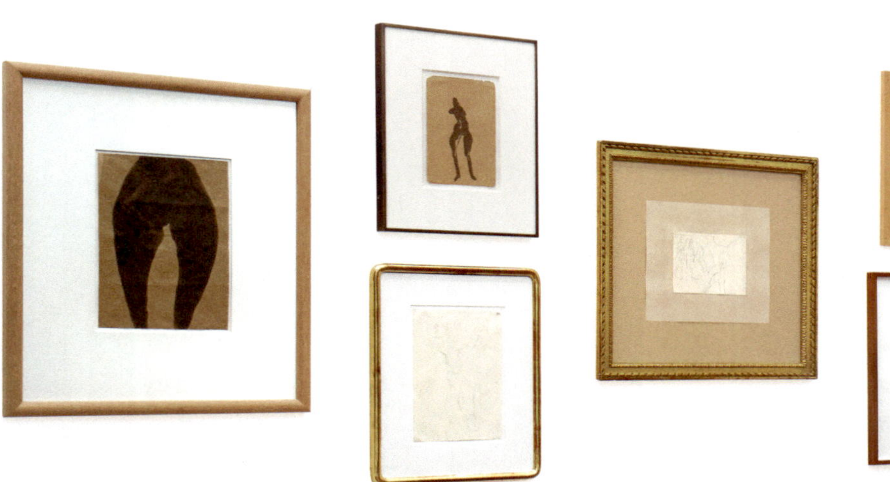

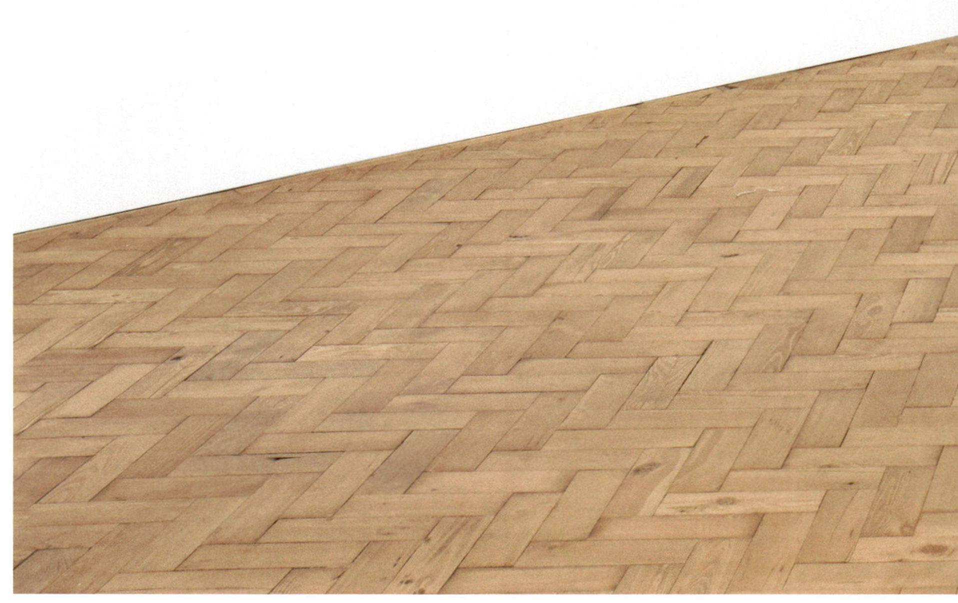

Rückenstütze eines feingliederigen Menschen (Hasentypus) aus dem 20. Jhdt. n. Chr. [Backrest of a fine-limbed person (hare-type) of the 20th century AD], 1972–82
Iron cast, vitrine
Backrest: 15 x 94 x 45 cm
(5.91 x 17.72 x 37.01 in)
Vitrine: 183.5 x 155 x 64.5 cm
(72.24 x 61.02 x 25.39 in)

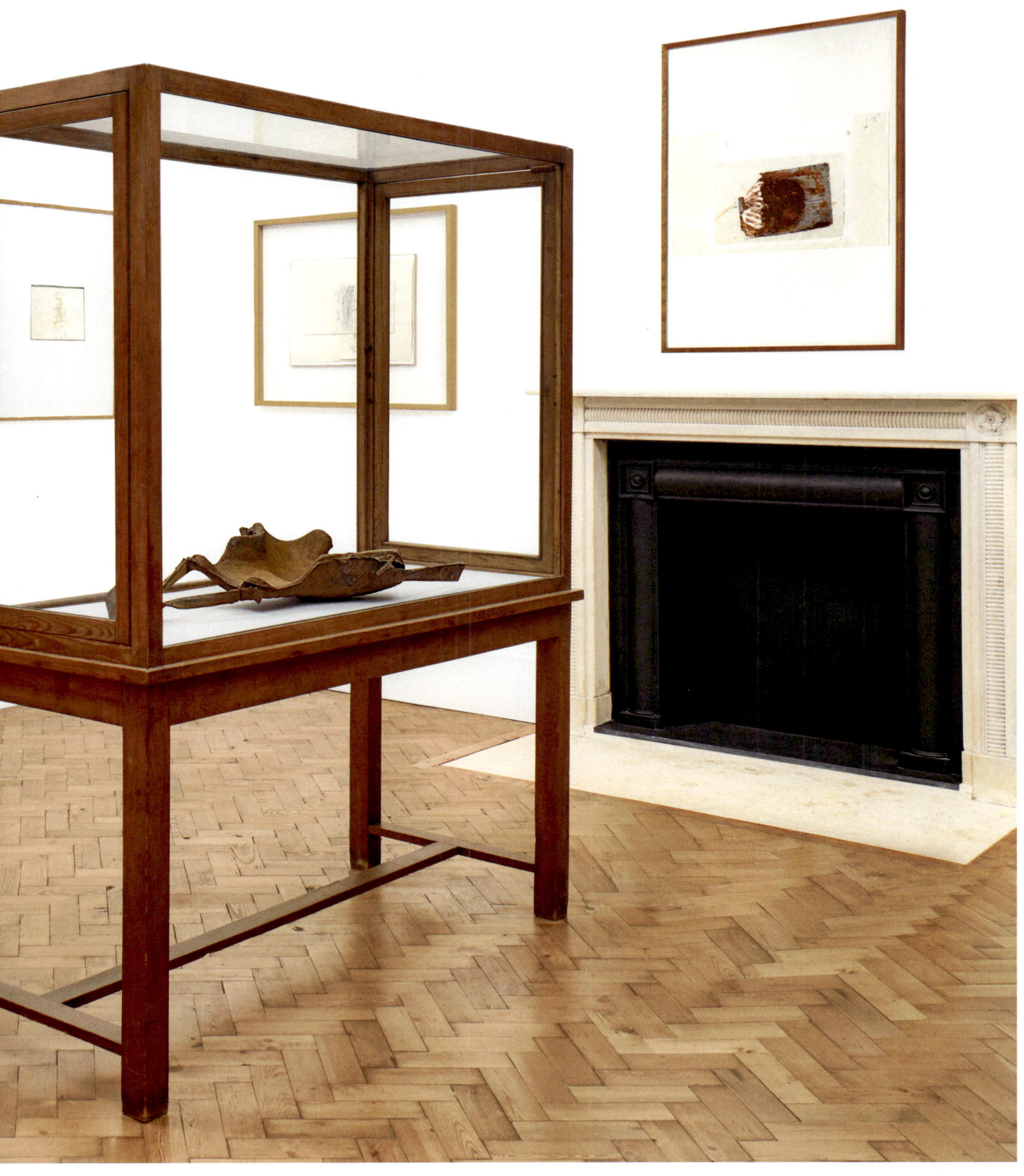

Joseph Beuys: Utopia at the Stag Monuments
Curated by Norman Rosenthal
17 April–16 June 2018
Galerie Thaddaeus Ropac London

Publisher: Galerie Thaddaeus Ropac
Artist Liaison: Xaver von Mentzingen
Text: Norman Rosenthal
Editors: Kelsey Corbett, Oona Doyle
Proof-reading: Olivia Baes, Claudia Pakula
Graphic Design: Simon Dara
Printing: Printmodel, Paris
ISBN 978-0-9957456-5-0
Print run: 1600

Galerie Thaddaeus Ropac
London
37 Dover Street
London W1S 4NJ, UK
Tel. +44 20 3813 8400

Galerie Thaddaeus Ropac
Paris Marais
7, rue Debelleyme
75003 Paris, France
Tel. +33 1 42 72 99 00

Galerie Thaddaeus Ropac
Paris Pantin
69, avenue Général Leclerc
93500 Pantin, France
Tel. +33 1 55 89 01 10

Galerie Thaddaeus Ropac
Salzburg
Mirabellplatz 2
5020 Salzburg, Austria
Tel. +43 662 881 39 30

www.ropac.net

Copyrights and credits

Figures
pp. 10, 13–15, 28: © Jochen Littkemann
p. 12: © bpk/Klaus Lehnartz
p. 16: © Helmut Wietz
pp. 18–19: © The State Hermitage Museum/
photo by Vladimir Terebenin, Daria Bobrova
p. 20: © Tom Carter
p. 22: Courtesy Joseph Beuys Estate
pp. 3, 23: © Estate Fritz Getlinger
p. 24: Photo RMN-Grand Palais (Musée
national Picasso-Paris)/René-Gabriel Ojéda
© Succession Picasso/DACS, London 2018
p. 26: © The National Gallery, London
p. 30: © Harald Thierlein
pp. 32–33: Translation of Joseph Beuys text
by Jeremy Adler originally published in
Zeitgeist International Art Exhibition, exh. cat.
(Weidenfeld & Nicholson, London, 1983).

Plates and installation views
Tom Carter: pp. 36–41, 46–51, 58–73, 82–95,
99–101, 108–109, 114–115, 119, 122–123, 133
Charles Duprat: pp. 87, 111–113, 117, 129, 156–161
Ulrich Ghezzi: pp. 44–45, 80–81, 126, 130–131,
135–137, 141, 147, 163
Marcus Leith: pp. 75–79
Prudence Cuming Associates Ltd: pp. 43, 53–59,
125, 127, 134, 138–139, 143–145, 149–155
Stephen White: pp. 96–97, 164–165

Set in *Albertus Nova®* and *Wolpe Pegasus™*
both of which were originally designed by
Berthold Wolpe and revived by Toshi Omagari.